Contributions to Economics

For further volumes
www.springer.com/series/1262

Piotr Pachura

Regional Cohesion

Effectiveness of Network Structures

Physica-Verlag

Piotr Pachura, PhD
Politechnika Częstochowska
ul. Dąbrowskiego 69
42-200 Częstochowa
Poland
piotrpachura@o2.pl

The research presented in this book was a part of a research project financed by grant of Polish Ministry of Science and High Education (Management and Network Economy - creation and transformation collaborative regional networks NN 115 3046 33)
ISSN 1431-1933
ISBN 978-3-7908-2809-2 e-ISBN 978-3-7908-2364-6
DOI 10.1007/978-3-7908-2364-6
Springer Heidelberg Dordrecht London New York

Cover design: SPi Publisher Services

Printed on acid-free paper

Physica-Verlag is a brand of Springer-Verlag Berlin Heidelberg
Springer-Verlag is a part of Springer Science+Business Media (www.springer.com)

To Aneta

Acknowledgements

This book would not have been possible without especially the valuable help of *Professor Maria Nowicka-Skowron*, Rector of *Częstochowa University of Technology*. For this, I express my heartfelt thanks.

Professor Jan K. Stachowicz (Silesian University of Technology) has been great and an innovative discussion partner. I have had numerous discussions with him and each time have learned. For this, I express my heartfelt thanks.

Doctor Tomasz Nitkiewicz and *Doctor Marcin Kozak*, my colleagues from *Częstochowa University of Technology*, have always supported me at my research. I express my warmest thanks to my colleagues for their in-depth, competent and valuable scientific discussions and help.

I have also obtained invaluable help from *Professor Ryszard Borowiecki (Crakow University of Economics)*, *Professor Edward Urbańczyk (The University of Szczecin)* and *Professor Maria Nowicka-Skowron* – my reviewers'. I express my deepest gratitude to them.

Piotr Pachura, Częstochowa, 2009

Contents

Chapter 1
Introduction – Thesis and Research Methodology

This book constitutes the results of research carried out with the aim of analysing the socio-economic cohesion of regions in the EU. The concept of research incorporates analysis of two dimensions of regional coherence:

- Dimension of the effectiveness of the transformation, particularly in connection with non-pecuniary factors of growth
- Dimension of regional networking

The aforementioned dimensions of cohesion were acknowledged as being very significant from the point of view of the development of the EU as a whole, as well as determining the elimination of the differences in the level of development of particular countries and regions, particularly in connection with the last enlargements (EU25 +2).

Simultaneously, the non-pecuniary factors of growth associated with the area of intellectual capital are becoming the main driving force of changes. However, networking as the illustration of a high level of social capital and potential of innovativeness is becoming the modern paradigm of development.

Empirical research carried out in this monograph involved the author's use of the adapted methodology for the analysis and assessment of the cohesion of regions in the EU in the context of the significance of the presence of network structures and the effectiveness of transformation in EU regions. The following assumption was accepted: "the level of networking in a region is the factor conditioning the effectiveness of the transformation."

The aim of the research was the verification of the following hypothesis: the occurrence of the relation between the efficiency of transformation and the degree of network interaction in EU regions that constitutes the dimension of socio-economic cohesion.

It was assumed that effective regions should possess a high degree of networking, but however in less effective regions the level of network interaction is lower. As a result of the research, a division of the group regions was carried out depending on the indicators of efficiency and the indicator of networking/clustering of

P. Pachura, *Regional Cohesion*, Contributions to Economics,
DOI 10.1007/978-3-7908-2364-6_1, © Springer-Verlag Berlin Heidelberg 2010

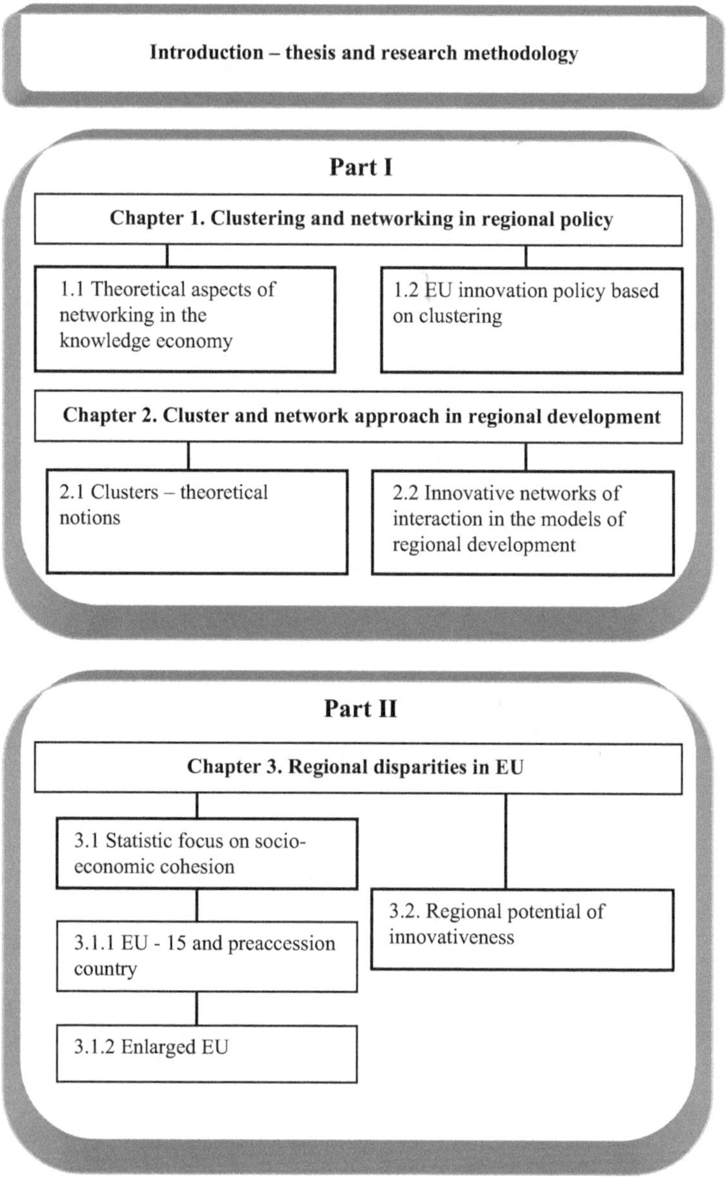

Fig. 1.1 (Continued)

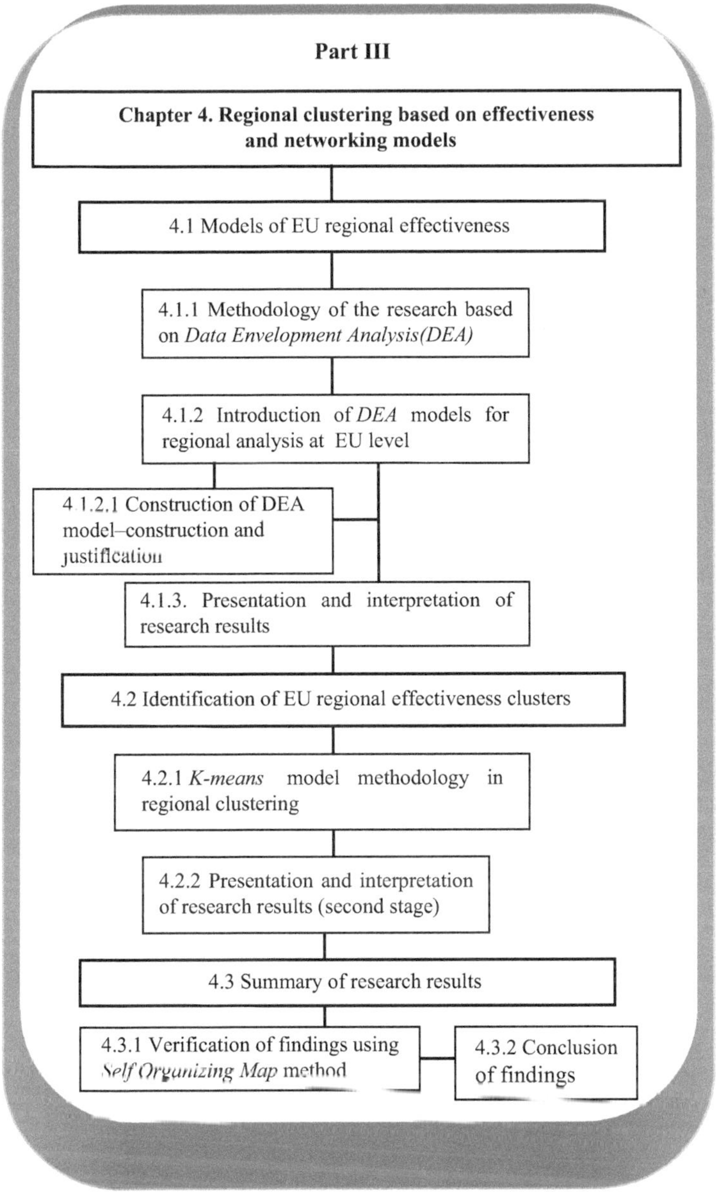

Fig. 1.1 Structure of the dissertation

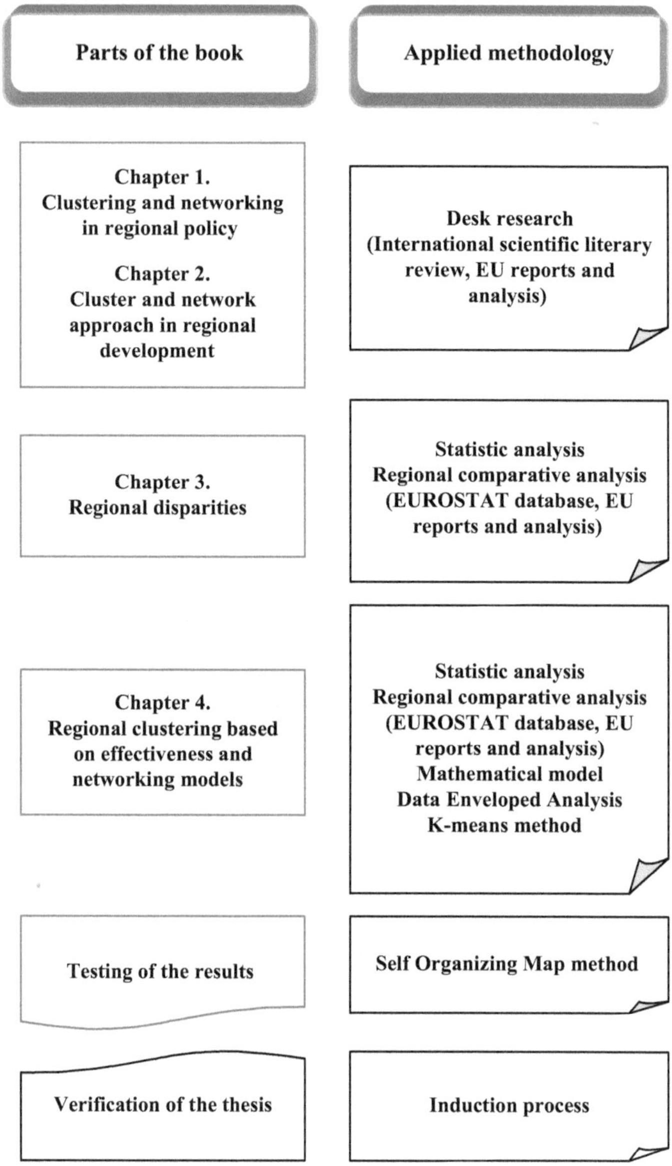

Fig. 1.2 Research scheme

regions which constitutes a contribution to the analysis of the socio-economic cohesion of spatial arrangements in the territory of the EU.

With the aim of verifying the accepted assumptions of the research a complex methodology was applied consisting of the following: *Data Envelopment Analysis*, *K-Means Models*, *Self Organizing Map*.

The data of regional statistics used in the calculations comes from the *Eurostat* publications, mainly the Fourth Report on the topic of cohesion in 2007, as well as the data from the *Cluster Observatory*. The calculations were carried out with the aid of MS Excel and special software including the programme called EMS Efficiency Measurement 1.3.0 (developed in TU Dortmund) and Gene Cluster 2.0 (developed in Stanford University).

The work consists of three fundamental parts matching the cognitive process with a deductive nature. In the following chapters the role of the parts with the nature of empirical research rises in importance.

The first part is devoted to the aspects of clustering and networking in a epistemological notion and in the dimension of the significance of this phenomenon in the processes of regional development. The first part consists of two chapters: *Clustering and Networking in Regional Development* and *Cluster and Network Approach in Regional Development.*

The second part of the monograph consists of one chapter entitled: *Regional Disparities in EU*, which presents the characteristics and statistical dimension of variation in the level of development in the territory of the EU. In this part of the dissertation we can find the characteristics of the variation of the EU both in the period prior to (EU 15) and following (EU 27) the expansion of the EU. The last part of the chapter is the analysis of the potential of innovativeness of EU regions as the fundamental factor generating socio-economic growth.

The final fundamental part of the book is devoted to empirical research on the basis of mathematical modelling with the aid of the methodology of the *Data Envelopment Analysis (DEA),* as well as the methods of clustering models. The third part consists of one chapter which is also the most extensive and is entitled: *Regional Clustering Based on Effectiveness and Networking Models* presenting the successive stages of research and their results. The final part of this paper consists of the analysis of the research results in the context of verifying the accepted research hypothesis.

In Figs. 1.1 and 1.2 the structure of the book is presented (Fig. 1.1) including the division into parts and the chapters and sub-chapters, as well as the research scheme (Fig. 1.2) presenting the research methods applied in particular parts of the book.

Chapter 2
Clustering and Networking in Regional Policy

2.1 Theoretical Aspects of Networking in the Knowledge Economy

The approach to the development and competitiveness of regions can be seen on the basis of examining economic concepts, starting from classic economics (Smith, Ricardo). In the classic economic theories, competitiveness was associated with the phenomenon of the *division of labour* which provides for economies of scale and differences in productivity across nations.[1] In the concept by Ricardo on the basis of the phenomenon of *comparative advantage,* the fundamental meaning connected with competitiveness referred to the benefits of international trade gained by particular countries.[2] Similarly, in neo-classical theory trade is deemed to be the engine of growth. Furthermore, it is deemed that free trade will equalise the prices of output, goods and, in turn, the prices of the factors of production (capital and labour) will also be equalised between countries.

Whereas classic economists treated capital and labour as two independent production factors, the Keynesian theory assumes capital and labour to be complementary. The Keynesian theory assumes that governments can successfully intervene in the cycles of the economy. This theory is of greater importance in the case of the policy of creating competitiveness of regions as state interventionism is evident and the convergence of regions can be achieved through economic policy.

In more contemporary theories of macro-economics, it is possible to find many more references to the question of shaping the competitiveness of regions. In the concept of *development economics* which is associated with *centre-periphery models,* the competitive advantage of "central" regions is most often rather long lasting and is catching up in terms of productivity which in the case of the 'central' and 'peripheral' regions is a slow process.[3] As *development economics theorems*

[1]Smith (2008).

[2]Ricardo (1957).

[3]Keeble (1976).

P. Pachura, *Regional Cohesion*, Contributions to Economics,

DOI 10.1007/978-3-7908-2364-6_2, © Springer-Verlag Berlin Heidelberg 2010

underline the lack of balance in the development of regions, foreign direct investment is of great significance in the process of convergence as regards regions. Economic policy plays an important role in determining regional success.

In the past decades the theory based on accumulation and the use of knowledge, frequently called the *endogenous growth theory* has been popular. Endogenous growth theory purports to provide a theory of economic history, in the sense that it tries to explain why some economies have succeeded and others have failed. The key assumption of the endogenous growth theory is that the accumulation of knowledge generates technological progress and economic growth. It is therefore acknowledged that investments in human capital and research and development are crucial for regional endogenous development.[4] The consequences for policy makers are for instance, the balance between spreading knowledge on the one hand, and protecting intellectual property rights on the other, in order to maintain the level of investments in R&D.

Aside from the theory on a macro-economic level, there are many theories associated with the explanation of the phenomenon of competitiveness operating at a micro-economic level which is of an interdisciplinary nature and is associated with such disciplines as sociology or economic geography. One of the most influential theories is Michael Porter's *cluster theory*. This theory is based on local competitiveness and the context of the global economy.[5] In accordance with this theory, in order to be competitive, an organization must continually improve the operational effectiveness of their activities and simultaneously strategic positions in the global economy. This assumption leads to the necessity of running a business activity at a local level while at the same time accepting a strategy of competitiveness at a global level – the effect of which is the creation of geographical clusters.

Another approach to the creation of competitiveness in a region is that which is based on the theories of economic geography, particularly the theory of locating business activities. The *Marshallian industrial districts* and the theorems of the economies of location are worth mentioning here. The formation of localized concentrations of industrial specialization is a part of the organic and organizational development of the industrial economy.[6] Marshall attributed the competitive success of key industries to their tendency towards geographical localization, and in turn industrial specialization as key to local economic success. Specialized industrial localization – consisting of various interactions fostered by inter-firm specialization and division of labour, the growth in the number of specialist suppliers, intermediaries – serves to reduce transaction costs, and promotes competitive advantage in the local production system. Furthermore, in this approach, knowledge and know-how are accumulated and become locally socialized into a local industrial "culture" and local "innovative environment." In contemporary times, the

[4]Aghion et al. (1998).

[5]Karlsson (2008).

[6]Cainelli and Zoboli (2004).

phenomenon of the *collective learning processes* is also underlined as the creation and application of innovative and entrepreneurial knowledge for the creation of a regional economic advantage.

Collective learning processes are simultaneously becoming a factor in the creation of the system of knowledge in a region, as well as an element in the process of creating a vision and aims for developing a region. Furthermore, with regard to the variety of approaches and interests of particular groups of regional players (institutional, business, social etc.), the common activity constitutes an element in the creation of trust as an element in the social capital of a region.[7]

Innovation is seen as an interactive learning process that requires interactions between a range of private and public regional players. The abilities of a firm to adapt innovation and knowledge are determined by its surroundings: its partners, competitors, customers, the human capital available, the regional knowledge infrastructure and institutions.

The increasing significance of the processes of knowledge and high level of IT in the modern market has become the stimulus for the shaping of such notions as: an economy powered by knowledge, information economy, information society, which is generally used with the aim of systemizing the phenomena that started in the 1950s. The arrival of a new era in the history of economic development – an economy based on knowledge, forced the players on the European and global markets to change their way of thinking to that of socio-economic activity, particularly in the area of gaining competitive advantage and striving towards socio-economic coherence by integrating the spatial structure. The necessity of adjusting to the conditions of a new economy was encountered by global corporations, individual enterprises functioning on a regional scale, as well as local authorities responsible for the shaping of regional policy in response to the new challenges of a global knowledge economy.

An economy based on knowledge is one directly based on production, distribution and the use of knowledge and information.[8] The notion of a *knowledge-based economy* should be understood first and foremost, as the definition of a modern stage of economic development, where knowledge is understood as the ability to act and play a decisive role in stimulating social and economic development.[9] Such an approach to the interpretation of this notion seems to be appropriate and allows us to notice that knowledge had been an important factor of economic growth prior to the emergence of economic models that are directly involved with knowledge as the fundamental factor of economic development.[10]

The knowledge economy is seen by the World Bank in a similar way, which defines this notion of a market availing of knowledge as the key engine of economic growth. It is an economy in which knowledge is acquired, created, spread and

[7]Cross and Israelit (2000).

[8]The knowledge-based economy (1996, p. 7).

[9]Innowacje i transfer technologii. Słownik pojęć (2005, p. 57).

[10]Jelonek (2004).

effectively used with the aim of supporting economic development.[11] The proposed theoretical concepts concerning the knowledge market are first and foremost aimed at explaining the roles of knowledge-derived resources and activities in stimulating productivity and economic development. Factors conditioning the economic success of enterprises and countries are much more dependent on the abilities of creating and using knowledge than ever before.

The necessity of referring to the essence of the knowledge economy is due to the attempt to set the appropriate context for the considerations at hand, as the natural attribute of the knowledge economy is understood in the wide ranging scope of a *network paradigm*. Therefore, it appears to be justifiable to define the modern economy as a network economy. On one hand, the modern economic area is being filled with network ties in global terms, but at the same time the role of local networks which constitute a defence mechanism against the negative effects of economic globalization.

The competitive potential of an enterprises is the function of the resources accumulated in the network in which the enterprises participates, the position it occupies in the network, as well as the abilities to mobilize these resources.[12] This is a notion that is representative of the economic concept of M. Bratnicki, that is seen as a specific form of interactions between various economic units in which the enterprises in question, as a part of the whole gain an advantage in the flexibility of activities and increase their competitiveness. The author defines the notion in economic terms as "the geographical concentration of mutually connected enterprises and institutions in a given area of business which represent a new type of spatial organization located between risk and hierarchy."[13]

The network organization is a modern form of organization that illustrates the way of organizing mutual ties between firms or units of an individual enterprise. Its existence was possible thanks to the reduction of transaction and transportation costs as a result of the resolution in telecommunication and forwarding technologies. However, the network organization also means a new style of management and a new form of organizing relations between companies. The fundamental basis for the ties between the network elements is at least the partial collectively of the aims, the realization for which particular elements voluntarily entered the network as network elements. Such a network can be formed by separating and significant independence of the elements of the organization or a combination of small organizations whose independent operations would be too problematic to maintain its position on the market. In this way they combine to increase their competitive strength by being able to counteract the activities of even large corporations.

From a theoretical point of view, the network constitutes an unquestioned hierarchy as a way of regulating events. Striving towards the reduction in the significance of the hierarchy as a mechanism for regulating activities and

[11]Chen and Dahlman (2006, p. 4).

[12]Sławecki (2005, p. 322).

[13]Bratnicki (1999, p. 22) and Sławecki (2005, p. 322).

integrating the organization causes the replacement of vertical communications and ties of giving orders and checking by horizontal ties. In such an organization the creation of an interpersonal network between employees is promoted, which supports the processes of the corporation. Thanks to the weakening hierarchical dependence and structures of the authorities, the level of flexibility and adjustability, as well as support for entrepreneurship are all increasing. The interactions between the elements of the network structures are therefore nothing more than channels of direct communications for people focused on a task and not authority. This facilitates the fast acquisition of knowledge and the multiplicity and mutuality of the transmission of information is the basis of cooperation and existence of the network. The interactions between partners and market mechanisms constitute an integrating element and external competitive pressure on the part of the organization that wants to connect with the network which causes the reduction of the prices offered for goods and services between partners. Such a solution favours the reduction of general costs and increases profitability by increasing competitiveness. The partnership of a network organization is based on mutual trust, common ideology and reputation. The discrediting of these elements can lead to the exclusion of a partner from the network or even the disintegration of the network itself.

In the afore-mentioned statement the interpretation of the knowledge economy by M. Castells is applied, in which in his opinion this market describes three mutually connected aspects: firstly, it is an economy concentrated on knowledge and information as the basis of production, productivity and competitiveness of both enterprises and whole regions, cities and countries. Secondly, an economy based on efficiency derived from knowledge and information which is global. The third factor which is essentially associated with the two previous ones is that of the *network economy organization*. These are decentralized networks from within enterprises, between enterprises and the networks of SMEs of dependent enterprises (subsidiaries of large corporations). In such an economy thanks to the networks, it is possible to facilitate extraordinary levels of flexibility and ease of adjustment. Therefore, it is an information based, global and organized economy within a network, in which one element can not function without the other.[14]

The *network* can be acknowledged to be a particular set (collection) of autonomous organizations that possess direct or indirect relations resulting from agreements (alliances) between the group participants. The purpose of the network is to gain a competitive advantage for particular participants of the network and frequently for the network as a whole. The feature of the network is the possibility of defining its borders (although frequently difficult), whereas the key phenomenon in defining the network is that the relations between enterprises within the network are greater than the relations between members of the network and external organizations (with relation to the network). Another characteristic feature of the network is the independence of the network organization members and their autonomous economic aims, which can be achieved thanks to participation in the network.

[14]Castells (2001) and Rózga Luter (2004, p. 31).

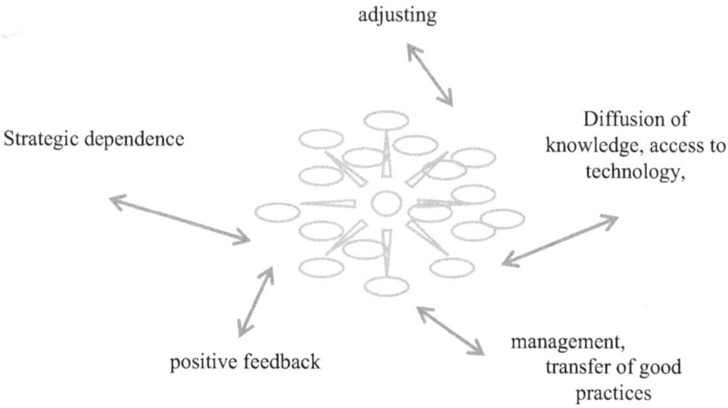

Fig. 2.1 Elements of the "*Network effect*"

The key phenomenon that occurs in the network is the *network effect,* or in other words, the impact (negative or positive) of the network on particular members (organizations, enterprises). The *network effect* can involve the following phenomena (Fig. 2.1): strategic dependence involving the restriction of strategic choices of the network participants; selection of partners resulting from the "adjustment" (*network fit/network fitness*),[15] diffusion of knowledge within the framework of the network (referring to good practices, particularly in the sphere of management); minimization of technological risk (participation in the network provides better opportunities of availing of the leading technologies); *positive feedback* which means for instance, availing of the economies of scale.

In accordance with the concept of *networking* an enterprise should possess an increasing level of abilities to cooperate with external partners such as universities, research units, or competitors that possess special skills. External cooperation facilitates the access to resources of particular knowledge which can be generated by internal structures of individual organizations. The network of cooperating units constitutes a central location of innovation as it provides knowledge and other inaccessible resources for individually operating organizations at the right time.

The dynamic ability to learn in an organization which generates a competitive advantage should therefore transgress organizational barriers. The functioning of the organization within the network of inter-organizational ties is seen as an important element in the organizational process of learning as the units learn through cooperation with others, as well as observation and adopting good practices from others. Enterprises do not gain their skills in isolation but discover, assess and learn from their implementation during the course of cooperating with partners of exchange. The ability of the organization to compete is the quality function of international ties and the learning abilities provided.

---

[15]Concept of *network fitness* presented by among others, Ard-Pieter de Man, Koen Franken and others.

The functioning of the enterprises within the framework of inter-organizational networks of cooperation brings specific results in the area of their innovativeness. The ability to generate innovation through cooperating organizations is to a large extent dependent on the type of ties and position held in the network. The value of the enterprise comes from its participation in the network, but however, the amount of social capital accessible for companies is determined by its position within the structures of the network. Therefore, the organization can gain value through the ability to create and use the knowledge acquired thanks to participation in the network. The network structure is defined by appropriate mechanisms and types of interactions which have an impact on the quality of relations and simultaneously, on the value gained by the organization.

Analysis of the mechanisms and factors of creating network structures of interaction and their transformation have great significance for the effective management of development of enterprises (participants or future participants of the network of interaction), regions and countries. The main course of research for network structures is associated with analysis carried out from the point of view of an enterprise (or a network participant in general). Scientific work is less advanced in the case of the mechanisms of creating and transforming networks in a spatial sense, as well as comparative research on the aspect of creating and transforming the network structures in various regions/countries with the aim of identifying the factors of success of particular participants of the network and the network itself.

It is increasingly stated that the notion of innovation includes everything that is connected with the creation and application of new knowledge with the aim of achieving a comparative advantage. In this sense, innovations apart from technology of course refer to economics, society and culture. Traditional approaches of science towards organization and management are insufficient to explain and manage the development of enterprises, as well as regions and countries. The modern economy called post-capitalist by P. Drucker requires a new approach to the challenges of development as the "individual act of innovation" which is no longer sufficient as innovation must be of a continuous nature. Therefore the core of the modern economy is becoming the network structure. The feature creating the network ties is most often their spontaneous and chaotic nature. With relation to this, a large role is attributed to the administrative environment as a "catalyst" and participant of the network of interaction. Moving away from the way of thinking that defines innovation as a linear process: science (basic research) – innovation (initiation) – commercialization, the direction of the paradigm of *continuous innovations (innovativeness)* requires a different view, frequently radical changes in thinking. If innovativeness is the following: constant process of the flow of knowledge and its creation, then the factors defining the effective functioning of the network structures are becoming more significant. Another important phenomenon associated with the change of innovative strategies of enterprises is the approach to the inspired concept of "*open innovation*."[16] Innovative strategies of enterprises up

[16]Davenport et al. (2006).

Fig. 2.2 The closed innovation model

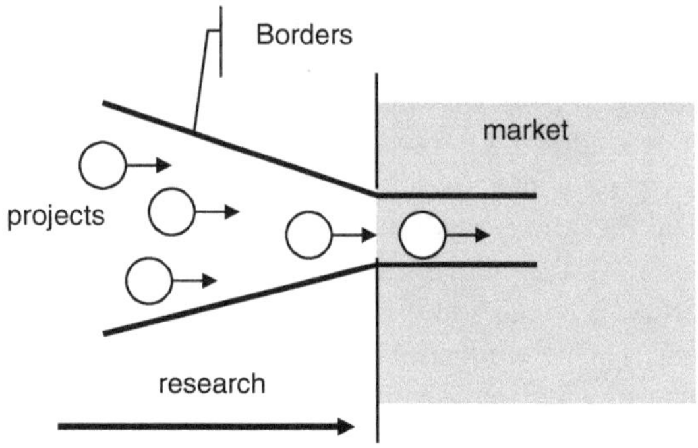

Fig. 2.3 The open innovation model

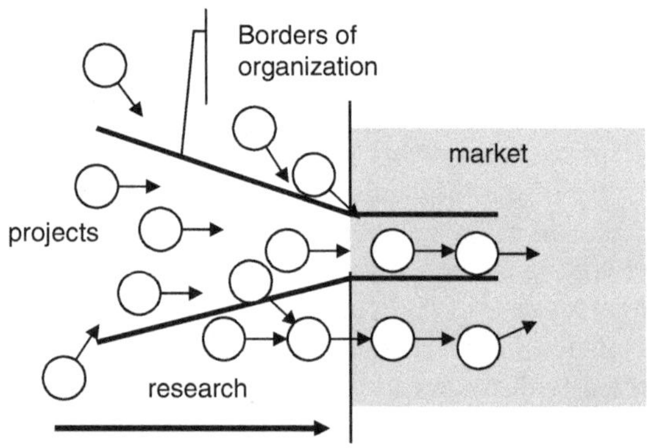

to now have been most frequently based on research on new products or services carried out by the enterprises themselves in their own R&D centres (Fig. 2.2). However, the concept presented in Fig. 2.3 defines a new model of creating and commercializing innovations based on a free flowing transfer of knowledge and innovation through the organizational borders of an enterprise. This model is most often based on network structures of interaction.

If we also assume that the *networking* itself is sufficient for the creation of the process of *continuous innovations*, but the quality of cooperation in the network (*quality of interactions*) then the category of social capital appears as a factor which stimulates the quality and effectiveness of the innovation.[17]

In the last few years, particular significance has been attached to the approach to pro-innovative network structures from the point of view of a region on the basis of the process of creating clusters.[18] Such an approach can be justified by the following: the possibility of locating certain elements of the network (geographical

[17]Nowicka Skowron et al. (2006).

[18]Particularly evident in the strategic development of voivodships and regional innovation strategies (RIS).

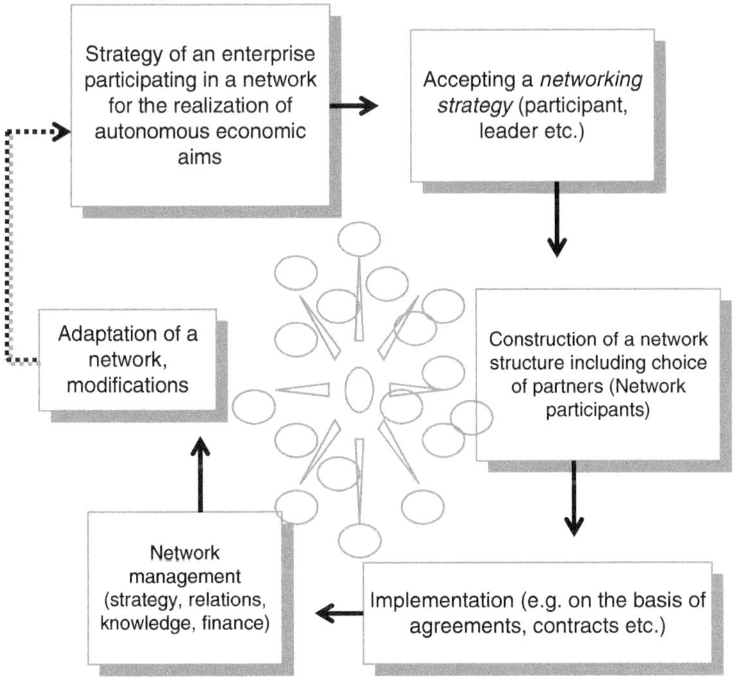

Fig. 2.4 Process of networking

proximity); direct contacts between the players is possible and can be created; synergy exists in the community of activity on behalf of the specified community and territory, as well as most frequently common psychological and cultural patterns.

However, from the point of view of innovative strategies of enterprises it is possible to speak of a *network strategy*, understood as a sequence of strategic choices (Fig. 2.4) associated with entering the network (or its creation) for the realization of autonomous economic aims. The stages of the process of *networking* includes the construction of network structures that involves a selection of the network participants, while subsequently the implementation or in other words, initiating the functioning of the network which most frequently takes place on the basis of agreements, contracts etc. (e.g., with relation to alliances or clusters, networks of course exist without the formation of formal agreements). Further stages are associated with the use of mechanisms, tools serving the management of the network and the adaptation of the functioning of the network to the conditions and changes in the network environment.

Innovation (innovativeness) is not (or is not only) a technical process of transforming knowledge into a new product or a process that requires the involvement of a social sphere. The dynamic dimension of the process of innovation can involve viewing the innovative network as a system which has the ability of self creation/auto-creation/innovation on the basis of key elements/dimensions (Fig. 2.5).

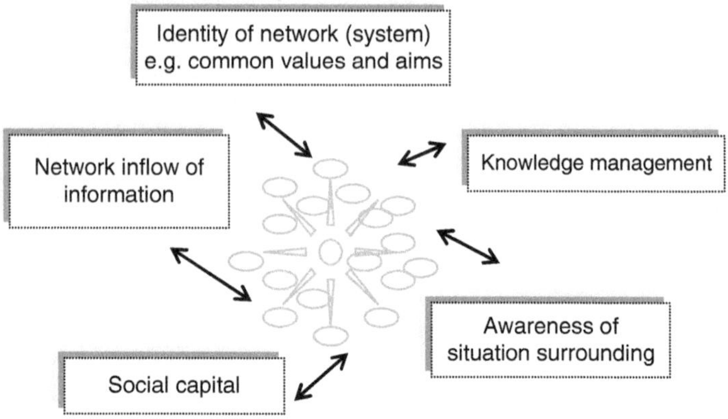

Fig. 2.5 Strategic network elements of an innovative nature

The system possesses features of distinction from the external environment and possesses the ability to provide an identity and justification of existence. It can also possess a common system of values. Furthermore, the identity of the players (elements) of the system is defined by the relations with reference to the external environment. The system of common values is created by external relations (between players) and relations with the external environment. The innovative system has the ability of "self maintenance" through the processing of information about its condition, changes emerging in the system, aims and principles of activity and cooperation. Constant communication and the flow of information must exist between the elements of the system (players), whose content is the identity of the system. Furthermore, the identity of the system is decided by the autonomy of particular participants (elements, players) of the network, as well as the conviction, consciousness of belonging to the network in question.[19]

The engine of the network is the mutual relations between the players, who avail of their participation in the network in an equal manner. The whole system must be seen by each player and simultaneously each one becomes partly responsible for the whole. The essence of networking can be understood as a varied system of relations (particularly from the view of personnel) within the framework of the network. Trust and tolerance also exist as the foundations of the flow of information and feedback.

Management of knowledge, the flow of information is the imminent feature of a system that is based on the appropriate tools for the transfer of knowledge and information flows. In this sense, the system is open to external information that flows in from the environment of the system. This system exists as "information flows" and is in a state of permanent uncertainty[20] which causes a change in the way of thinking and breaks up routines. The phenomenon of entropy is associated with

[19]Pachura and Kozak (2006).

[20]Prigogine and Stengers (1984).

the surplus of information and their disorder constitutes a factor that stimulates the formation of a new" synthesis of knowledge which leads to innovativeness. The innovative system on one hand, creates an entropy of information and knowledge on the other hand, restricts and strives towards ordering and directing their use in the realization of these goals. We are therefore faced with the phase (state) of the entropy of knowledge and its ordering (crystallization) in the second phase. In the network, there must be acceptance of the surplus of information and tolerance to the mistakes and uncertainty among the players.

It is worth mentioning that the process of knowledge management in innovative strategies can be based on the classic cognitive concept that is based on the analysis and processing of information relating to in an objective manner the existing external world concepts of organized knowledge, *autopoiesis*, or in other words, dynamic knowledge created within the framework of the organization itself.[21] The theory of *autopoiesis* in terms of an organization is to a certain extent associated with the theory of the emergence of systems and in this case in the system which possesses the properties of emergence the knowledge of *autopoiesis* can be known as the expression of the emergence of the system.[22] An innovative system constantly functions between chaos (*disorder*) and order (*crystallization*). The knowledge relating to taking decisions is important with relation to the external environment. Analysis of the environment and knowledge of the processes occurring outside the network is of significant meaning in taking decisions on the aims and strategies realized by the system. Recognising the opportunities and threats facilitates the efficient realization of aims.

Taking the conditioning of the global knowledge economy into consideration, it is possible to distinguish the strategic determinants of development as regards network structures of interaction. It should be treated as a platform or its own type of "fertile soil," on which the concept of networking grew that is understood as the formation of various forms of interaction from the centres of technology transfer, to clusters, and finally regional systems of innovation.

The fast changes emerging in the competitive environment of enterprises and at the same time the key role of innovation in gaining economic benefits is the characteristic feature of the period of the knowledge economy. That is why, it is suggested that instead of the term the knowledge economy, the term the *learning economy* should be used, as it fully reflects the changes occurring. The fast tempo of change means that specialized knowledge is becoming a resource that has a shorter life cycle and from this the ability of learning and adapting to new conditions to a large extent determine the results of individual units, enterprises, regions and countries.[23] *The organizational aspect of learning as a critical factor in generating innovations constitutes the basis for creating interaction ties and is currently first and foremost at the level of network interactions within the framework of the*

[21]Stachowicz (2006).

[22]Pachura (2006).

[23]Lundvall and Borrás (1997, p. 31).

concept of clusters. Therefore, the use of the term the learning economy is justified in the context of interpreting the phenomenon of networking in a spatial dimension. Enterprises strive to achieve interaction even with their competitors at the cost of losing part of their market share, but in order to achieve the strategic aim of gaining valuable knowledge from other units. The *geographical proximity* is seen to be significant here, as well as the external effects of networking in the form of *knowledge spillovers*, which stimulate the process of clustering.

The significant meaning of geographical proximity determining the realization of the processes of knowledge in the region is the common element of the models of regional development thought up with the aim of constructing regions based on knowledge. According to Cooke, the potential resulting from geographical proximity is materialized through the exploration and use of knowledge while taking account of the open channels of knowledge which are important for these processes. These channels offer a wide range of possibilities for expanding the potential of knowledge as it can lead to "information leaks" resulting from the geographical proximity.[24] Research observations referring to the role of knowledge in the development of the spatial arrangement mainly take account of the *knowledge spillovers* and the creation of regional innovative centres in which the spatial proximity to the creation and sharing of knowledge is crucial.

Both in the case of clusters and other types of regional innovative centres the ability of innovative location and the process of the network itself emerging are based on the phenomenon of the *localized knowledge spillovers* and availing of the benefits of the functioning source of valued knowledge in the defined spatial proximity by the units themselves. The knowledge spillover occurs in the situation where knowledge that is created by a given unit leads to the creation of knowledge or innovation by other units. In this concept, the assumption that the creation of new knowledge brings positive external effects is key. These effects take place as knowledge is not an exclusive product and is difficult to exercise total personal control on it.[25] A. Francik defines these effects as the "uncontrolled process of the penetration of knowledge and its products, as well as various types of skills."[26] The author further underlines the essential role of these types of effects with relation to the systems of innovation and underlines that the essential role should be attributed to the flow of knowledge on the basis of informal contacts between the participants of the regional systems, as the efficient transfer of knowledge is difficult to code and first and foremost takes place through inter-personal relations. The deepening specialization of a region is becoming the source of endogenic development based on the internal intellectual potential of growth.[27]

The information flows resulting from geographical proximity are acknowledged to be one of the most important factors in the creation and development of clusters,

---

[24]Cooke (2006, p. 24).

[25]Greunz (2005, p. 451).

[26]Francik (2003, p. 93).

[27]Francik (2003, p. 93).

particularly those concentrating the innovative enterprises.[28] The main aspect in the statement underlining the large significance of information flows in the region with relation to the process of networking is the fact that the transfer of new information takes place in a way which is more effective between units that are located close together. The essence of spatial proximity in the successful realization of information flows results from the basic properties of knowledge associated with the activities of innovative firms, mainly their complex nature and detailed nature of *tacit knowledge*.

The currently binding model of innovation forces the observation of the process of creating knowledge in the dimension of a system or in other words, a network. The new theory of economic growth forces cooperation in the area of realising the processes of knowledge, which has led to the binding *network paradigm of innovativeness*. In traditional economic models which explain the theory of economic growth, knowledge and technology remained as external factors. A significant change in this interpretation occurred thanks to the acknowledgement of technology as a key and endogenic factor of growth, the effect of which the *Total Factor Productivity (TFP)* was introduced, thanks to which the impact of innovation on the growth of productivity was reflected. This theory which was worked out by Solowa – a laureate of the Nobel Prize underlined the meaning of technology in the function of production, which in turn commenced research on knowledge as a factor driving the growth of the economy. As opposed to the neoclassic theories of growth, knowledge is becoming recognised as an endogenic factor of growth within the framework of the new theory of economic growth (*new growth theory*).[29]

The process of creating knowledge understood as the process of innovation is an interactive process which incorporates the interactions between organizations specialized in the creation of knowledge, enterprises, financial institutions, consumers and suppliers. As a result of the binding model, innovativeness is becoming regional and domestic systems of innovation are concentrating cooperating units together – as participants of the process of innovation. That is also why the process of creating knowledge can be defined as the interactive process which is of an organic nature. The modern growth of resources in terms of knowledge is taking on the features of a non-linear process.

Issues relating to the recreation of knowledge and the process of transferring knowledge conditioning its use in the economy, while also recognising the essence and role of transferring and spreading knowledge on a regional dimension led to the increased interest in regional concepts of networks of knowledge and innovative systems responsible for the realization of the afore-mentioned processes. In associated literature and strategic principles formed at the level of EU institutions, the essence of transferring technological knowledge from the sector of science and research to the economy is discussed at length. With relation to this, the meaning of

[28]Hoen (2001, p. 3) and Breschi and Malerba (2007, p. 2).

[29]Lipsey (1999), Abramowitz (1989), Nelson and Winter (1982), Arrow (1962), and Romer (1990).

close interaction between colleges and the world of science with that of business is emphasized as this favours the process of transferring technology.[30] Therefore, the regional possibilities in the area of R&D activities are associated with production operations within the framework of one regional system of innovation. With the aim of stimulating the processes of transferring technology various mechanisms of interaction are initiated such as technological centres, technology transfer centres and technological incubators.

The necessity of making organizational interaction results from the essence of knowledge, or in more precise terms, one of its categories – *know-how*. This comes from the industrial sector where it defines the skills and abilities that are not described with the aid of patents and licences, but technology transfer which is crucial at a given moment. This type of knowledge is usually developed and maintained within organizational limits of an individual enterprise or research team. However, together with the growth in the complexity of knowledge the trend towards development of interaction between organizations occurs. One of the most important reasons for creating the network of enterprises is actually the need to gain the possibilities of combining and sharing the elements of the complex type of knowledge known as *know-how*. Similar networks that are created are between research teams and laboratories.[31]

The ability of creating innovation should be understood in accordance with the dynamic and interactive model of the process of innovation. *Innovation is understood here as a process of a network and systemic nature, in which innovations are the result of numerous and complex interactions between units, organizations and the environment.* Innovation is the process of learning, which means that it is the result of accumulating specific knowledge and information that is useful for the activities of enterprises. The process of innovation uses internal and external sources, which makes it an interactive process.[32] The systemic approach to innovation means the impact of the widely understood external institutional players on the innovative activities of enterprises. The systemic notion of the process of innovation underlines the essence of transfer and diffusion with regard to categories of knowledge and skills. Flows of knowledge take place within the framework of channels and networks situated in a socio-cultural environment that has an impact on the innovative abilities of the regional players. Innovation is seen as a dynamic process in which knowledge is accumulated through the processes of learning and interaction.[33]

The innovative ability of a region – understood in the categories of a systemic organ is determined as the ability of networking and collective learning. The systemic approach to innovation provided the beginning of the concept of creating new mechanisms of regional development. The central point of the innovative

[30]Goldberg (2004, p. 14).

[31]Knowledge management in the learning society, as above, p. 15.

[32]Stawasz (2005, pp. 39–40).

[33]Oslo manual. Guidelines for collecting and interpreting innovation data (2005, p. 33).

management of a region became the issue of cooperation and interactive processes of creating, diffusion and applying the knowledge by the regional players. The establishment of the systemic approach is mainly reflected in the domestic models and regional systems of innovation, concepts of learning regions, innovative clusters, or the local innovative environment. The basis of the shaped concepts of regional development is that of the *network paradigm of innovativeness*. The creation of regional networks of interaction facilitates the mutual learning of the participants of the process of innovation and strengthens the flexibility of mutual activity. A particular role is also played by the social aspects of the innovative processes, which often take their course in accordance with unwritten principles and cultural traditions and explain the processes of networking.

Most concepts that are written into the systemic approach to innovativeness in a spatial dimension are based on regional network interaction that incorporates units representing the sphere of business, institutional environment and units of the scientific and research sphere. The development of regions based on knowledge and innovativeness constitutes a layer of related models of learning regions, local innovative environment, clusters, or finally regional systems of innovation. The converging assumptions of these concepts are particularly related in the policies of regional development realized by EU member countries. The problematic of creating a competitive advantage on the basis of the pro-innovative networks of interaction became the subject of consideration for many modern theories of regional development. Innovativeness and knowledge of a region were acknowledged by many theories of regional development as the most important factors of a regional economy. They indicate how to build the competitiveness of a region on the basis of the endogenic potential of growth. The modern binding models of regional development emphasize the mobilization of internal potential of the growth of location, which is to be the source of a competitive advantage of spatial arrangements. The assumptions of related concepts are widely initiated in the case of learning regions, innovative clusters, innovative environments, entrepreneurial environments, or domestic and regional systems of innovation. The models of regional development based on endogenic and knowledge-derived growth potential illustrate the abilities of a region in the sphere of realizing the processes of innovation guaranteeing self-renewal in a globalized and fast changing economic environment.

2.2 EU Innovation Policy Based on Clustering

According to the afore-mentioned results of literary research it is possible to univocally state that the geographical proximity between enterprises of a similar profile of activity facilitates the achievement of a higher level of productivity and innovativeness. The clusters covering the spatial sphere of its location: producers, suppliers, service providers, research units, educational institutions and other units supporting a given sector became an important factor in the economic development of regions. The trend towards interaction and basing on the resources of business partners operating in a given location results from the new trends of management, among others, the school of resources in strategic management at the top with key competences and the *open innovation paradigm.*

Directing the regional policies of the EU along the concept of clusters also results from the wide impact of the progressing globalization on the essence of inter-regional competitiveness. Increasingly lower costs of transport and communication and the simultaneous liberalization of international trade revealed the weaknesses of regional economies and exposed them to global competition. With regard to the increasing number of locations with attractive conditions for investment, European regions faced the necessity of offering foreign investors even more unique benefits. Clusters became in this situation a magnet attracting a bunch of highly specialized resources of knowledge in a given sector which are not present in other locations.

Therefore, due to its practical application, the concept of the theoretical clusters regardless of whether the work of M. Porter or as a stage in the evolution of industrial districts of Marshall in the direction of the systems of innovation became one of the most important elements of economic, innovative and regional policies of the EU. The reasons for such a turnaround in the activities of the European Commission have been previously indicated. It is possible to add that the traditional instruments of supporting economic growth and the competitiveness of regions, for instance by supporting whole branches of the industrial sector, have not succeeded and had to be replaced by a mechanism that is more adjusted to the challenges of the global economy.

The network approach to innovation and the according theory of clusters became the central point of interest for the EU. A key element in the policies of innovation of the EU became the *cluster-based policy*. This type of policy is defined as a grouping of activities and instruments used by the authorities at various levels for the improvement of the level of competitiveness of the economy by stimulating the development of the existing cluster systems or their creation at first and foremost the regional level.[34] Among the elements that decide on the effectiveness of policies of supporting clusters the following assumptions can be listed[35]:

- The driving strength of the cluster policy is the free market
- This combines various units of the regional economy
- This is based on cooperation and mutual activity
- This takes the form of a strategic nature and helps to shape a common vision
- This creates new value

Involvement in initiating policies based on clusters can be naturally explained by the determination of EU member countries in the realization of the aims of the Lisbon Strategy whose achievement at the first deadline turned out to be impossible.

[34] Brodnicki et al. (2004).

[35] Cluster based economic development: a key to regional competitiveness (1997).

Clusters seem to be the appropriate direction for the realization of the innovative policies of the EU. From the point of view of the European Commission, promoting policies based on clusters is to lead to the achievement of the aims of the Lisbon Strategy. The competing conglomeration of enterprises provides the possibility of access to the network filled with skills and abilities to generate innovation. They are becoming an effective environment in which it is easier to realize the initiation of new products immediately after their development in research laboratories.

A policy based on clusters is not a separate element of activities on the part of national and regional authorities, but should be rather treated as an integral element of various policies. This is most frequently reflected in the assumptions of scientific policy or scientific and technological, innovative, economic, and regional development. In this way the idea of clusters penetrates into the strategy of development for regions, but is also taken into account in state programmes that are financed by the EU structural funds. Most often however, the philosophy of policies based on clusters takes on a horizontal nature and finds itself in all the afore-mentioned policies. It fits in perfectly into the policies of regional development based on the model of the innovation system. Clusters as a way of arousing the innovativeness of regions usually find themselves among the priorities of regional strategies of innovation. The cluster policy is part of the model of strengthening interactions within the framework of the so-called *triple helix*, or in other words, the system of interactions between the key players of the system of innovation: enterprises, scientific and research units and local authorities.

The concept of clusters became a topic of interest for national and regional governments, organizations of entrepreneurs, international organizations particularly OECD countries and the EU in the second half of the 1990s. This interest can be observed through successive *cluster initiatives*, starting from the theoretical work explaining the essence of clusters to the attempts of working out the methodology of their identification and finally the guiding rules in the sphere of the policies of stimulating clusters in regions. These last initiatives are worth devoting more time to in order to illustrate the factors of success in undertaking activities within the framework of regional policies on behalf of the development of clusters, which has been done in the later stages of this paper. The guiding rules of the programme and the strategic documents of the EU took account of the concept of clusters relatively late as it occurred at the beginning of this century but it is necessary to explain this as a rather different approach to the issue of the innovativeness of regions. The efforts in this area were from the very beginning directed towards the issue of the systems of innovation, industrial districts and local innovative environments, which in their own essence are also based on the network paradigm of innovativeness.

Apart from the initiation of the afore-mentioned models of regional development, another trend of activity in the EU associated with clusters was the creation of networks of interaction between regions. The stimulation of networks of interaction appears in various aspects and policies of the EU. The scientific and research policies can be used here as an example together with its main instrument in the form of the Framework Programmes that support the networks of interaction of scientific centres and their relations with industry. In the middle of the 1990s, the

EU started to place particular emphasis on the issue of regional innovativeness. The breakthrough moment was the passing of the Lisbon Declaration by the European Council in 2000 and the acceptance of the aim of transforming the EU economy in the most competitive market based on knowledge in the world. In this context the policy of supporting clusters in EU member countries grew in importance and the regional authorities acknowledged that the foundation of competitiveness is that of small enterprises. The creation of an environment that is friendly towards the development of small firms became a priority, particularly through the stimulation of interaction between them and also creating interaction with the R&D sector. The strategy of development for EU member countries initiated with the aid of programmes financed by EU funds that were assigned priorities in the sphere of supporting networks of interaction at the level of enterprises and the area of R&D. The network model of innovativeness was accepted as binding, in which the theory of clusters fits perfectly.

The activity of the EU Commission in the area of creating a favourable regulatory framework and the popularization of knowledge on the topic of clusters is confirmed by many conceptual papers and documents among which the following can be mentioned:

- "Industrial Policy in an Enlarged Europe" from 2002, in which the creation of innovative clusters became acknowledged as the key priority of the new industrial policy
- Communiqué entitled "Some Key Issues in Europe's Competitiveness – Towards an Integrated Approach," according to which one of the proposed activities was to be the European project of identifying the best practices in the sphere of initiatives of developing clusters
- Programme document entitled "Industrial Policy in an Enlarged Europe" from 2004, in which the innovative policies and supporting initiatives based on clusters were listed as being of key importance
- Consultation document entitled "Innovate for a competitive Europe," which states that the structural funds can support the internationalization of regional clusters, which according to the European Commission became the effective mechanism of stimulating innovation

The policy of regional development based on clusters can be the effect of bottom-up initiatives, as well as resulting from top-down initiatives. The second type of operation is the effect of the activity of the local authorities, however the bottom-up activity is usually characterized by the activity of the branch environment. Regardless of the way of realization of the cluster initiatives, a significant role should be attributed to the public authorities. According to M. Porter, the role of the public factor in creating and stimulating the development of the cluster in the area of shaping the factors of production, related and supporting sectors, conditions of demand, as well as the strategy and rivalry between enterprises.[36]

[36]Porter (2001).

The first paper that carried out a complex analysis on the effects of policies based on clusters realized in selected countries is the document entitled "*The Cluster Initiative Greenbook*."[37] In this document the results of research into cluster initiatives were presented within the dimension of their effectiveness and range. Interesting results were also presented within the framework of a range of OECD projects[38] directed at the analysis of practical aspects of the functioning of clusters. The afore-mentioned projects were aimed at diagnosing the existing state in the area of cluster initiatives, as well as working out the guiding principles in the area of formulating and initiating innovative policies based on networks. A compendium of knowledge and a type of guidebook on the topic of shaping policies based on clusters is constituted by the work prepared by the non-governmental organization IKED (*International Organization for Knowledge Economy and Enterprise Development*).[39] In the identification of the recommendations and factors of success in the realization of cluster initiatives the report prepared at the request of the Ministry of Trade and Industry of Great Britain was also used.[40]

On the basis of the afore-mentioned documents it is possible to indicate the experience of particular countries in the area of initiating policies based on clusters. The results of research facilitate the creation of the basic recommendations for the practical formulation and initiation of the policies of regional development based on the concept of clusters.

Cluster initiatives most frequently appear in highly developed countries, mainly in the sectors of large technological intensities with regard to the following: IT, telecommunications, medical equipment, production technology, pharmaceuticals, automotive. Most initiatives were directed at the development of a specific cluster and were started between the years 1999–2002. The aims of creating cluster initiatives are very varied and can be classified within the framework of the following six categories: research and the creation of network interactions, education and training, innovation and technology, expansion of cluster, political activity, commercial interaction. Within the framework of the distinguished categories of aims, most participants of clusters (over 75%) indicate the main aims of their participation in cluster initiatives as follows: the creation of interaction between enterprises and creating relations between people, development of their own company, easier access to new technologies and the ability to create innovation. Initiatives that have a priority goal in promoting innovation and new technology achieve significantly greater success in the area of improving the competitiveness of particular enterprises.

---

[37]The cluster initiative greenbook.

[38]Boosting innovation. The cluster approach (1999), Innovative clusters. Drivers of national innovation systems (2001), and Innovative networks. Co-operation in national innovation systems (2001).

[39]Andersson et al. (2004).

[40]A practical guide to cluster development, Department of Trade and Industry, DTI, London.

The process of creating and organizing cluster initiatives takes on different forms despite the fact that the nature of such initiatives enforces the principles of creating a partnership between the industrial sector, research and public authorities. The participation of particular parties is varied in individual cases. The idea of constructing a cluster is most frequently becoming an initiative of local authorities and the sector of enterprises at a more or less equal pace. A decidedly greater role in the aspect of financing cluster projects is played by public authorities. In over half of the clusters analysed, the main source of financing was the regional budget or national public units. In turn, the involvement of colleges in initiating clusters in their initial phase of development was very small, which clearly confirms the low financing coming from these units. A dominating role in managing clusters is played by the sector of enterprises, while the role of public authorities in some decisions is also envisaged. The involvement of local authorities, most often in the form of neutral organizational units, is to lead to the balancing of interests of the competing enterprises. The source of financing does not seem to have great significance in achieving results both in the aspect of competitiveness as well as the numbers of members of a cluster.

According to the theory of clustering, most initiatives are directed in their own sphere in a given industrial branch or geographical zone. Most existing clusters include units that are located within a radius of one hour's drive. The aspect of geographical distances was indicated as a significant factor in facilitating mutual personal contact. Clusters are not limited to the type of enterprises which can become its member. Both direct competitors and foreign business units can freely participate in the aforesaid initiatives. The only restriction in this regard refers to one level in the value chain, which means for instance a greater role in including specific producers but not their suppliers and clients.

The fundamentality of initiating policies based on clusters is becoming univocally confirmed by the benefits indicated which are provided to enterprises in these types of initiatives. Entrepreneurs identify the success resulting from the membership of a cluster through the prism of competitiveness and achievement of business goals. Most entrepreneurs confirm that the initiatives led to the improvement of their competitiveness and the most frequent effect is the tightening of interaction between the industrial sector and the R&D area. The factors that are decisive in the success of clusters include the following: the quality of the business environment, structure and way of running economic policies, as well as the internal strength of the cluster itself. Within the framework of the first category two key factors should be listed which attract other firms to participate in the cluster initiative to the highest degree: the presence of an advanced scientific society and a high level of trust between firms, while also the public and private sectors. Economic policy is also significant with such elements as: promotion of scientific research and innovation, the possibility of taking economic decisions at a regional level, protection of the high level of market competition. The trend of achieving better results in the area of competitiveness is visible through cluster initiatives directed at strong clusters. Clusters with a significant economic meaning on the scale of the whole region or country and a longer history of existence are more attractive for new members.

They usually attract the presence of enterprises that compete on an international scale.

Within the framework of research presented in the *Greenbook* a range of factors was diagnosed that are decisive to the failure of cluster initiatives. The greatest significance is attributed to the lack of consensus in the area of taking action, as well as a clearly formulated vision for the initiatives and undefined aims of a quantifiable nature. Significant meaning in the failure of initiatives is played by the issue of insufficient resources, both in infrastructure and financing. Other elements that lead to unsatisfactory results are as follows: restriction of the range of membership to only groups of large enterprises, one level in the value chain or enterprises belonging to the location dictated. Large significance in the failure of cluster initiatives is also played by a lack of trust in the initiatives undertaken by public authorities.

A survey of the reports prepared up to now on the topic of cluster initiatives in various countries enables us to note that the policy of supporting clusters takes on various forms. In reality it does not only vary from the level of analysis accepted and the methodology applied in supporting the process of networking, but also the degree in which the policy based on clusters was initiated, as well as the instruments used for this purpose. In terms of synthetic analysis, a set of strategies can be presented that was chosen by selected EU countries with relation to the ways of initiating policies based on clusters (Table 2.1).

The most frequent elements in the strategies of the development of clusters include:

- Strong competiveness of the economy and the reforms of economic policy in the area of market regulations
- Supplying strategic information by way of foresight type projects, cluster analysis and internet portals
- Agencies dealing in contacts with entrepreneurs and units supporting innovativeness e.g., innovation centres
- Development programmes for the development of clusters financed by public funds
- Establishment of centres of excellence connecting the industrial sector with the R&D area
- Adhering to public procurement (public tenders)
- Construction of platform for public and private dialogue

In many countries the process of clustering was initiated by the establishment of allowances, platform and regular meetings involving enterprises and organizations from the business environment associated with a given branch. The motive for starting dialogue was the results of research projects, particularly the technological foresight, which aroused discussion and prompted joint action. Generally speaking, the process of initiating clusters and other networks of interaction in a dimension of European regions takes on various forms depending on the political culture, way of institutionalizing the dialogue between the public sphere and the private sector, the size of the regional economy, but also depends on the scale of intervention of public

Table 2.1 Strategy of implementing policies based on clusters in chosen countries of the EU

Country	Approach	Cluster analysis	Policy initiatives/policy principles
Austria	Systems of interdependent economic entities	– Improving I/O tables – Traditional statistical cluster analysis screening for patterns of innovative activities – Case studies	– Cluster policy under construction – Framework conditions (regulatory reform, human capital development) – Providing platforms for cooperation and experimentation – Raising public awareness of technologies – Demand pull by public procurement
Belgium (Flanders)	Networks or chains of production, innovation and co-operation	– Graph analysis and case study work – Improving I/O statistics – Technology flows – Technology clubs (similar collaboration patterns)	– Cluster-based policy under construction – Market induced cluster initiatives – Government facilitating co-operation – Subsidies and co-financing for firms in cluster programmes (in metal processing industry, plastics, space industry, SMEs, furniture) – Stimulating cross-sectoral technology diffusion – Supporting supplier-producer networks – Centres of excellence around newly emerging technologies
Denmark	Resource areas	– Industrial districts/development blocks – Porter-like cluster studies – Improving statistics – Cluster analysis as an input to the process of dialogue	– Dialogue in reference groups – Centres of excellence in specific areas – New educational programmes in specific areas – Development centres in specific areas – Top down approach (selected priority fields) – Institutional reform in policy making (coordination between ministries)
Finland	Clusters as unique combination of firms tied together by knowledge and production flows	Porter-based cluster studies	– Clusters as an economic development tool – Identifying sources of competitive advantages in Finnish economy – Competition policy and structural reform – Creating advanced factors of production (basically creating favourable framework conditions)

			– Cluster programmes, strategic research, centres of excellence
Netherlands	Value chain approach	– Porter-like cluster studies – Cluster benchmark studies – Input-output analysis	– Dialogue in specific platforms – Brokerage and network policy – Public consultancy – Providing strategic information (a/o. technology foresight studies) – Renewal in procurement policy – Deregulation and competition policy
Spain	Inter-sectoral linkages and dependency	Technology and innovation flow analysis	– Framework policy – Stimulating R&D co-operation and R&D networks – Research centres (mixed private and public participation) and science parks
Sweden	Interdependencies between firms in different sectors	– Development blocks (1950s) – Technological systems (late 1980s) – Network approach (since the 1970s) – Porter studies (since the mid-1980s)	– Cluster-based policy under construction – General framework conditions – Technology procurement – Stimulating R&D cooperation – Research centres – Industrial systems project (is being set up) to stimulate strategic dialogue – Technology foresight studies – Identifying actual or potential innovative clusters
United Kingdom	Regional systems of innovation	Cluster case studies focus on identifying actors and development opportunities for the region	– Clusters as a regional development – Tool – Government as catalyst and broker – Regional cluster programmes

Source: Boosting innovation. The cluster approach (1999)

authorities in economic life, as well as the degree of industrial and technological specialization of the region.

In the afore-mentioned reports and expert analysis a set of key recommendations in the area of initiating policies based on clusters indicates the factors of success listed below[41]:

- The main role should be accepted by the sector of enterprises, however public authorities take on the role of a catalyst in the development of the cluster in question. In such an arrangement, the expansion of the public and private sector partnership is key
- The aims of the initiated policies should be transparent and measurable
- Clusters should be built on the basis of existing potential and avoid creating initiatives in branches which are not sufficiently developed or generally do not appear in a given location
- The presence of a large enterprise in a given branch which is seen positively as a source of new technologies, acquisition of expertise, client base and suppliers, as well as space for the development of human resources
- Adequate technical infrastructure is essential together with a developed network of transportation and telecommunication connections, as well as an accessible base of attractive real estate for investors. Institutional mechanisms are helpful here in the form of entrepreneurial incubators, scientific, technological and industrial centres, due to the conditions of mutual work in a specified physical space offered by them
- The presence of an entrepreneurial spirit, especially among employees of a scientific and research unit and large innovative enterprises which is to lead to the formation of spin-off and spin-out firms
- The possibilities of access to financial capital in the form of high risk capital (venture capital), networks of investors searching for innovative and prospering enterprises (the so-called business angels), loan funds and finally public programmes, finance programmes e.g., EU funds
- The development strategy of a cluster should be realized at an appropriate level of local government which facilitates the effective initiation
- In the initial phase of development of a cluster an analysis of the potential or existing concentration of enterprises of a given branch should be analysed making use of the existing clusters in other locations. The results of this analysis should be used for public debate with the aim of working out a wide social consensus
- The action taken should enable the increase in the specialization of cooperating enterprises and institutions with the aim of realizing economies of scale and range, division of labour, as well as development on a local scale of specialized factors of production which facilitates the strengthening of the competitive position of the cluster

[41]Worked out on the basis of the following: "Uwarunkowania rozwoju nowoczesnych technologii w Gdańsku" (Conditioning of development of modern technology in Gdansk), IBNGR, 2002.

- Using the benefits accruing from the geographical proximity should be promoted by the establishment of associations of sub-suppliers or other forms of mutual interaction (e.g., associations of mutual credit guarantees) stimulating diffusion of knowledge and technology, as well as the processes of mutual learning
- In the case of highly technological clusters, one of the fundamental activities should be acknowledged as stimulating and creating flexible interactions at the level of industry and the academic sector
- For the achievement of success, it is essential to build clusters on the basis of formal and informal networks of interaction within which the information flows can take place. This type of social network that emerged on the basis of a high level of trust and social capital can be stimulated by strong institutional structures divided by cultural values and common goals
- The market success of a cluster is conditioned by the access to the base of skills understood as the highly skilled workforce
- Mechanisms should be created that enable resignation from cluster initiatives in the case of their failure

In summing up, the results of the analysis of the conditioning of the initiated innovative policy directed at clusters, it should be first and foremost underlined that the key aim of this policy should be to strive towards the creation of a long lasting competitive advantage in the economy of the region. The way for achieving the afore-mentioned aim can become a strong innovative cluster or group of smaller innovative clusters functioning within the framework of a coherent system of innovation. The policy based on clusters should be supported by a set of other complementary actions within the framework of related policies, which leads to the gaining of synergy effects. This is therefore the policy which penetrates into other policies and in its own essence takes on a nature of horizontal activities. The concept of clusters is according to other models of development for innovative regions and should be treated in this way as a supplement for the models of the learning regions, regional systems of innovation and the innovative environment. All the afore-mentioned theories of regional development are based on the network paradigm of innovation and enable local spatial arrangements to meet the challenges of the global knowledge economy.

Chapter 3
Cluster and Network Approach in Regional Development

3.1 Clusters – Theoretical Assumption

An integral element of modern regional economies of the EU is that of network ties between the participants of economic life who are exceptionally successful at innovativeness and regional competitiveness. The significance of the innovative network is increased with the perspective of intervention undertaken within the framework of the EU structural policies. The changes in emphasis in the course of increasing pressure on innovativeness and development of new technology is evident, instead of the exclusive subsidies to poorer regions. The central role in increasing the competitiveness of EU regions with relation to the economies of USA and the fast growing economies of South East Asia, especially Japan and to an increasing degree China and India, is attributed to the construction of regional networks of sectoral interaction of enterprises. The network form of interaction is seen as the way to increase productivity and innovativeness.

In deliberations on the topic of regional networks of interaction, it is worth paying attention to the concept of clusters which can be acknowledged as one of the key elements in the development of regional systems of innovation. Regional clusters are characterized by a particularly advanced network structure and its significance is equally emphasized by the innovative policies of spatial arrangements. The concept of clusters, widely popularized in associated literature and already standardized in its initiation within the framework of the policies of developing EU regions is attributed the role of strengthening the regional innovative abilities. Clusters have become an integral part of regional systems of innovation and rather one of the conditions facilitating the shaping such systems in regions. This is the conditioning of the fundamental role that the process of clustering (or in other words, the spatial concentration of network structures[1]) plays in increasing competitiveness and innovativeness in local economies.

[1]Skowron-Grabowska and Otola (2006, pp. 55–65).

P. Pachura, *Regional Cohesion*, Contributions to Economics
DOI 10.1007/978-3-7908-2364-6_3, © Springer-Verlag Berlin Heidelberg 2010

The theory holds true where it states that the situation where European regions will fall behind with regard to defined categories of clusters with relation to their equivalents on the scale of the world economy can become a significant factor in the low competitiveness of the regions in a global economy. This particularly refers to the new EU member countries in which the previous centralized economy system enforced top-down location of entire industrial branches regardless of their possible effectiveness. Cluster structures in these countries significantly differ in the level of development and experience in the sphere of increasing competitiveness.

In associated literature there are many varied definitions and ways of interpreting of the notion of clusters and also ones which do not refer to the issue directly but univocally relate to the characteristic features of a cluster or in other words, the simultaneous competitiveness and interaction. Therefore, it is possible to speak of many related theoretical concepts which are based on common features that evolved over the past decades. However, the most widespread and most implemented in economic practice has been the theory referred to by M. Porter as clusters. Nevertheless, it should be underlined that the assumptions of Porter were not a total novelty, but in their essence referred to the already described related concepts indicating the significance of the concentrations of enterprises from one branch in a defined spatial location (industrial districts of Marshall, the Italian industrial districts, the French *filierie* and mezosystems, new industrial spaces according to the Californian school).

According to the definitions of clusters provided by M. Porter, they are "geographic concentrations of mutually connected firms, specialized suppliers, units providing services, firms operating on related sectors and their associated institutions (e.g. universities, units of normalization and branch associations) in particular areas competing against each other but also cooperating."[2] The idea of clusters is included by Porter into one of his well known concepts of the diamond of competitiveness within the peak of the related and supporting sectors.

The main idea is the assumption that for the diamond which is made up of particular groups of factors to function as an efficient system, it is necessary for spatial concentration and rivalry between enterprises of the same sector to exist. The concentration of competing firms, suppliers, clients and very frequently scientific and research units lead to the increase of productivity, specialization and accelerate the processes of innovation. As a result, "the trademark of the region" is created which attracts qualified employees and foreign investors. The given location becomes a unique environment of the specified industrial sector.

In the aforementioned definition most interpretations of the notion of clusters quoted in international reports are included. For instance, it is possible to quote one of these which defines a cluster as a geographical concentration of mutually connected enterprises of related branches, specialized suppliers, service providers and their associated institutions (universities, branch agencies and trade associations), which simultaneously compete and cooperate with each other.[3]

[2]Porter (2001, p. 246).

[3]Biotechnology Clusters (1999).

In turn, P. Cooke states that the aforementioned definitions reflect an assumption of a cluster which is too static and the interpretation of the notion should reflect its dynamic nature. Therefore, the author proposes a different definition by taking account of the future vision of the given cluster that is shared by firms. Cooke defines a cluster as firms of a close proximity that are connected by vertical and horizontal relations, incorporating local infrastructure of support for enterprises and sharing the future vision of development based on competition and interaction on a specified market area.[4] Such an interpretation of clusters brings us closer to the manner of understanding them with the theories of systems of innovation whose precursor is actually P. Cooke.

There is a fundamental agreement in the area of the categories of units creating the network interaction within the framework of clusters. Among the main players it is necessary to list enterprises, public institutions, scientific and research units and financial institutions. Particularly important in this context from the point of view of the success of cluster initiatives is the active role of institutions of animators, who stimulate the process of interaction in the network (Institutions for Collaboration[5]). The role of particular players is different depending on the specific local conditions and the phase of the life cycle of the cluster in question.

As in the case of defining the notion of a cluster, in the dimension of categorization there is no single model that carries out a commonly acknowledged systematic analysis of the types of clusters. According to a report prepared at the request of the Ministry of Trade and Industry in Great Britain, the structure of a cluster can take on the following forms:[6]

- Chain of added value – the core of the cluster constitutes neighboring enterprises in the chain of added value; vertical interactions in production processes have fundamental meaning in this case
- Aggregation of the connected sectors – large scale type cluster distinguished by M. Porter as being composed of four fundamental parts: the production segment of final products, production of machines and equipment, specialized outlays and supporting services
- Regional clusters – the aggregation of connected sectors concentrated in a spatial sense within the framework of the region in question which conditions its global competitiveness
- Industrial districts – local concentration of SMEs specialized in particular stages of the production process, strongly associated with the local environment, on the basis of trust and cooperation ties
- Network – specific form of connections between economic players on the basis of interdependencies, cooperation and trust (but does not have to be spatially concentrated)

[4]Cooke (2001, p. 24).

[5]Andersson (2004).

[6]"*Uwarunkowania rozwoju nowoczesnych technologii w Gdańsku*" (Conditioning for development of modern technology in Gdansk), IBNGR, 2002.

- Innovative environment – synergy of economic and institutional factors in the areas of highly technological industries that lead to the effective creation and diffusion of knowledge, as well as the effective process of learning

In current literature there is also a classification based on existing structures in network cluster interactions. On the basis of this criteria the following types of clusters are distinguished:[7]

- Related clusters of the Italian industrial districts of which the best example is the American Silicon Valley. These are characterized by the domination of SMEs, strong specialization, mutual rivalry and the simultaneous system of network interactions based on trust
- Clusters of the hub-and-spoke type which are characterized by co-existence on a given territory of a large enterprise connected in a hierarchical form with a wide ranging group of SMEs (e.g. Seattle – Boeing and Toyota City)
- Satellite clusters with a dominating share of SMEs, which are dependent on external firms and their advantage in terms of the location is mainly based on the cost advantage (e.g. Research Triangle Park in North Carolina, USA)

Cluster structures do not form in an economic vacuum but grow on the basis of specified socio-economic conditions in a given location. There is a set of defined factors that are acknowledged to be the determinants of the development of clusters, although there is a lack of consensus in literature about their significance for the stimulation of the process of clustering. While being conscious of the multiple factors indicated and their varied constellation, it is possible to distinguish several fundamental classifications which appear most often in literature. In examining these factors it is important to remember that there are no standard models of clusters and univocal factors that decide on their efficiency or success. The features listed below are of various weight or importance depending on the location of the cluster, its profile, phases in the life cycle, as well as maturity and amount of network interaction.

Taking account of the factors of developing successful clusters quoted in literature, it is possible to divide them into the following three groups:[8]

- Critical factors of success: partnership in the network, strong base of innovation with the support of R&D institutions, human capital, historical and cultural conditioning, high level of trust between the participants of network ties
- Factors supporting success: appropriate physical infrastructure, presence of large enterprises, strong corporate culture, access to sources of financing and services that support entrepreneurship

---

[7]Szultka (2004).

[8]Groups of factors of development for clusters was proposed as a result of the literary research carried out and presented in the following publication: "A Practical Guide to Cluster Development," Department of Trade and Industry, DTI, London.

- Complementary factors of success: competition, access to information, leadership, external economic influences

The dependence between any given factor and the successful development of clusters was not proven. They are to a more or less degree present in the successful clusters. Nevertheless, the fundamental meaning in the context of developing the clusters can be attributed to social resources, which are mainly classified as elements of social capital. The impact of socio-cultural conditioning for the development of network ties was observed by Marshall and Becattini who thoroughly examined the processes of functioning in the production centres in specified territorial areas. G. Becattini in analysing the phenomenon of dynamic development of regions of the Third Italy defined it as a social and territorial unit. He pointed out that the success of these regions is conditioned by tradition and local ties based on mutual trust.[9]

The role of social capital appears in both the initial stage of the formation of a cluster, as well as in the phase of its development in the dimension of interaction between units in the network. Mutual trust and the culture of entrepreneurship and interaction are becoming key to the success of a cluster, which are strategic factors in constituting the creation of social capital. The social aspect of successfully functioning cluster structures appears in a unique way in the process of formulating the strategy of clusters where the common consensus is required for the vision of its activities. This is also the critical factor from the point of view of the innovative abilities of clusters. That is why, it is worth devoting this aspect more consideration.

The social context of the functioning of clusters is highly individual at the level of each region, which does not allow for the direct transfer of the tried and trusted solutions without regard for the historical, cultural and institutional factors. Each individual cluster is an exceptional structure that is deeply built into the local specific conditions. The strong sense of taking root as regards this system in the social conditions of a given region constitutes the basic criteria that differentiates the particular clusters. The non-economic factors to a large extent explain the mechanisms of formulating systems of network interaction.

In this case, the assumptions formulated by Scott and Storper would seem to be accurate, in which they mark out the role of non-economic factors in regional development. Scott saw an essential role in two factors of the innovative development of a region; the appropriate policies of public authorities and social and cultural conditions. Particular emphasis was placed on the role of the network interaction of various institutions, as well as the unwritten social norms that encourage entrepreneurship, competition and risk taking. In the opinion of Scott, economic development depends to a great deal on "specific economic institutions and social norms that occur in the region other than invisible market forces."[10] The main conclusion coming from the research carried out by the author is that every

[9]Becattini (1990).
[10]Scott (1993).

agglomeration should create its own model of institutions and social behavior, which would ensure its competitive advantage in the best possible way.[11]

Scott defines non-economic factors of regional development as *untraded interdependencies* that occur between the participants of the economic activity. The untraded interdependencies in their meaning transgress the traditional economic transactions on the basis of formally regulated exchange. In the same way, they incorporate interactions on the local labor market, business environment, shared norms, customs and values, as well as practices in the area of communication and interpretation of knowledge.[12] Formal and informal rules of social life in the form of norms of behavior and customs constitute a set of principles that reduce economic risk and increase the level of entrepreneurship and can support mutual cooperation. In the case of territorial concentration, the untraded interdependencies are becoming a key factor in the creation of innovative structures that favor learning and the development of an innovative region.[13]

Regardless of the varied factors of development and accepted approach to the theory of clusters, the characteristic features that are not commonly emphasized in associated literature can be indicated as follows:

- Concentration on a defined geographical area of interdependent enterprises and other cooperating business units (scientific and research institutions, public organizations, branch institutions), which belong to related industrial branches
- Interactions and functional ties between enterprises
- Horizontal ties (complementary goods and services) and vertical (chains of purchasing and selling)
- Simultaneous competing and cooperation within the framework of the aforementioned groups of interaction which is defined in the English language as co-opetition (from the words cooperation and competition)

In turn, there is rather a consensus among researchers as to the benefits which the current system of clusters brings to the region. It is difficult to provide a detailed analysis of all the effects which the functioning of clusters brings to a regional economy and individual enterprises. They have been empirically described in detail in research projects and several key beneficial effects have been provided below which have been indicated by most researchers:[14]

- The growth of productivity of local enterprises due to the access to relatively cheap and specialized factors of production
- The increased innovativeness of units located within geographical proximity
- The increased competitive advantage of enterprises located in cluster structures
- The creation of new work places thanks to the dynamism of development of the cluster and the formation of new enterprises

---

[11]Grosse (2002, p. 39).

[12]Salmi et al. (2001, p. 29).

[13]Pollock (2003, p. 15).

[14]Department of Trade and Industry, DTI, London; Hoen (2001); Szultka (2004).

- Positive effects of external effects (the so-called spillovers) in forms of among others, the increased access to specialized services, modern technology, infrastructural investment
- Possibility of combining the complementary skills with the aim of gaining more advanced orders, which would not be possible to do by an individual enterprise due to the low price competitiveness
- Wider range of possibilities of using the effects of economies of scale by the following: enhanced specialization of each firm, joint purchases of greater amounts of raw materials at lower prices, joint marketing activity
- Strengthening the social interaction and other less formal contacts, which can lead to the formation of new ideas and the establishment of new enterprises
- More effective channels of information flows within the framework of networks of enterprises and institutions of the business environment, which can favor for instance, an easier evaluation of trustworthiness by business partners and financial institutions

It is worth paying more attention to the issue of competitiveness and innovativeness which seem to be the most significant factors from the perspective of using clusters as a tool of regional development policies. Thanks to the beneficial effects of developing cluster initiatives, regional development policies in European regions can lead to the expected results in the area of constructing the most competitive knowledge economy in the world.

Therefore, it is particularly important to assign clusters with the role of strengthening the regional innovative abilities, of which the effect is the identification of them from the notion of innovative networks. Empirical analysis has shown that the clusters feature a high level of innovativeness and competitiveness. Porter notes this feature of clusters and emphasizes that the close ties with business partners to a large degree lead to the tempo of perfection and innovation. Clusters have an impact on the competitive position of enterprises by indicating the direction and pace of innovation. The existing relations of firms within the cluster with other units help them to gain the knowledge on the topic of new technologies, possibilities of acquiring new components and machines within an appropriate timescale, as well as other areas of activities for enterprises. The process of learning is aided by facilitating visits to enterprises and frequent personal contact. As a result, clusters provide the abilities of flexible and fast reaction to changes.[15] Geographical proximity and frequent direct contacts facilitating the observation of other firms operating in a cluster gives the opportunity to observe the trends among buyers faster than in the case of firms operating in isolation. Furthermore, competing firms are forced to make themselves distinct in a creative way against the background of the other business units in the cluster.[16]

[15]Porter (1998, p. 83).

[16]Porter (1998, p. 277).

Thanks to the spatial proximity and network interaction between firms in the cluster, synergy appears between sectors and knowledge is accumulated that is appropriate for a given industrial centre. This knowledge decides on the abilities of the clusters to generate the breakthrough innovations which can lead to the formation of new sectors.[17] The basic attribute of clusters in the form of the geographical proximity of enterprises is a factor of particularly significant meaning in the case of fundamental technological change. In the case of radical technological change, new technologies that have not yet been documented are becoming accessible in the form of tacit knowledge. In this situation, personal contacts that are facilitated thanks to the proximity of enterprises are key to the exchange of this type of knowledge. The significance of proximity seems to be lower in the case of gradual technological changes as this type of innovation requires codified knowledge more, thus enabling the ease of transfer over long distances. In effect, the theory presented that clusters are becoming more valuable for firms or developing new technologies than for firms based on gradual innovations.[18]

The condition which is essential for the formulation of the strategy of regional development based on clusters is their thorough analysis, which is to lead to the establishment of an exit route and the diagnosing of the potential for the creation of clusters. A wide range of research methodology is at our disposal, starting from quantitative research, to the study of individual cases and finishing with the detailed qualitative research and analysis of the network. It is difficult to indicate the most appropriate methodizes as the efficiency depends on the individual aims of the research. Researching clusters can however serve not only the formation of strategy regarding their development in a specified area, but it is also becoming the supporting tool in carrying out a comparative analysis of regions. By accepting the criteria of positioning regions in terms of degrees of concentration in the cluster structures, it is possible to monitor the policies of coherence that are realized in the regions. The theory which is accepted as being justified here is that the greater concentrations of network interactions in the form of clusters in a given area creates the potential of competitiveness and innovativeness in the local economy. The diagnosis of the regional economies through the prism of clusters can serve as tools in assessing the competitive potential. This is entirely in accordance with the theory of clusters proposed by M. Porter who made them into research tools of the competitive advantage of spatial arrangements. In this type of research, methods based on the coefficient of location are deemed to be more adequate. They are based on statistical data and are actually due to the nature of comparative analysis among a large group of territorial units.

The listed statistical coefficients illustrate the concentrations that occur in a given region of specified industrial branches and services. The listed coefficients can appear in the use of various statistical variables e.g. the number of people employed in enterprises of one branch, the amount of revenue from sales or the

[17]Gancarczyk and Gancarczyk (2002, p. 81).

[18]Hoen (2001, p. 11).

amount of exports. The main disadvantage of this kind of methodology is the inability to diagnose interdependencies and the amount of interaction between units of a given cluster. However, taking account of the aims of the research, the aforementioned failure does not constitute serious obstacles in gaining the desired results.

The methodology of identifying clusters (mapping) by statistical analysis based on the indicators of location were successfully applied by M. Porter[19] and are widely used in similar comparative analysis of clusters on a interregional scale. The basis of the methodizes of Porter is the analyses of employment in particular industrial branches and subsequently the assessment of their co-existence in selected regions by analysis of correlations in pairs. In the first step, the local branches are separated from the branches which are of significance in external exchange with other economic areas. Local branches do not have a strong spatial concentration of employment and can be distributed with the use of statistical methods. In the following stage the strength of exports in the case of particular branches is analyzed. Branches competing abroad are combined and their interaction is identified by the research of correlation in terms of employment between regions. Subsequently, the spatial borders of a region are marked out in the analysis of the table of branch flows and definitions of branches. Finally, the identified clusters of industrial branches competing on a supra-regional basis can be marked out on a map on condition that their indicator of location is higher than one. After gaining the results, it is possible to run a wide range of comparative analysis between regions e.g. in the area of overlapping clusters or relations between clusters and the level of economic development of the location.

3.2 Innovative Networks of Interaction in the Models of Regional Development

Most concepts entered into the systemic trend towards innovativeness are based on regional network interactions in a spatial sense. They incorporate units representing the sphere of business, institutional and the scientific and research environment. The development of regions based on knowledge and innovativeness constitutes a level for related models of learning regions, local innovative environment, clusters, or finally, regional systems of innovation. Converging assumptions of these concepts are particularly reflected in the policies of regional development realized by EU member countries.

[19]The author carried out thorough empirical research on 700 clusters within the framework of 50 countries in the Cluster Meta-Study project: www.isc.hbs.edu. The detailed metodology of the cluster analysis which was used by M. Porter was presented in the paper: "Business Clusters in the UK," Department of Trade and Industry, DTI, UK, 2001.

The models exposing the role of knowledge and innovation to a large extent get their inspiration from the evolutionary output of economics, evolutionary theory of technological changes, as well as new theories of innovation assuming a non-linear nature of the process of innovation.[20] This topic was initially undertaken by the Nordic school which introduced the term of the learning economy. According to it, the keys to these processes are learning and transferring knowledge, sharing knowledge and creating innovation, interaction and trust arising from the cultural context and the local environment. The Nordic school also underlines that the spatial essence of the proximity of firms and units facilitates the accumulation of knowledge and the associated innovation, as well as the transfer of knowledge between players of a given location. This particularly refers to tacit knowledge that is based on experience. The pro-development element is also emphasized here in the form of a system of relations. "Innovation and knowledge are systemic and collective and only operate in the complex system of firms connected together in a network of interaction and institutions. Therefore, the role of social networks and local institutions is decisive in this process."[21] As a result of research on such a system on a national scale, the term of the national system of innovation was introduced which subsequently as a result of further work evolved in the direction of the concept of a regional system of innovation.

The motive of the local system that favors the creation of knowledge and innovation was developed in the research work carried out within the framework of the GREMI group (*Groupe de Recherche Européen sur les Milieux Innovateurs*), which introduced *the model of the local innovative environment* as an incubator of innovation and the self supporting "knowledge machine." The main assumption of the concept of the innovative environment is the claim that the source of innovation is not that of enterprises, but first and foremost the local environment where it functions. The innovative environment was defined as a structure or in other words, a complex network of mainly informal social relations that exist on a defined area and is determined by the sense of belonging, local culture and customs. This type of structure of an organic nature strengthens local innovativeness and the collective process of learning.[22] Innovativeness is seen as the integration of information and resources by the local environment. One of the elements of the innovative environment is that of the strong territorial and institutional structures, which create an instrument which is essential for the process of managing and creating an environment associated with learning. The most important point of interest in innovative environments is the maintenance of local synergies. From this, the territory is seen as both the reason and the effect of the synergies of players and the collective

[20] Olejniczak (2003, pp. 59–60).

[21] Asheim and Isaksen (2000); Olejniczak (2003, p. 60).

[22] Olejniczak K., "Unia Europejska i Organizacja Współpracy i Rozwoju Gospodarczego wobec gron" (European Union and Organisation of Cooperation and Economic Development with regard to the community) Szultka S., edit. "Klastry. Innowacyjne wyzwanie dla Polski" (Clusters. Innovative challenges for Poland), IBNGR, p. 19.

processes of learning.[23] Further work on the concept of the innovative environment bore fruit in the appearance of a more profound and practical use of the theories of regional systems of innovation.

Further approaches emphasizing the fact that the factors of competitiveness of enterprises first and foremost emerge in conditions of regional development and are referred to as *learning regions*. The dominating role of knowledge in regional development was observed by such authors as: Florida, Morgan, Cooke, Lundvall, who led to the spread of the notion of a learning region in literature. The main driving force of the learning region is that of constant innovation and the ability to adapt to changing market conditions. This means the role of public authorities whose opinion should be stimulated by all the factors responsible for the development of science, research, improvement of personnel and the application of high technology in the enterprises of the learning region.[24]

According to OECD, the model of the learning region guides the direction in which the regions should strive towards with the aim of a successful reaction to the challenges resulting from the emerging learning economies. For the learning region, the key is the ability to be flexible and maintain interaction including the exchange of knowledge between various units of the region in the face of changing economic conditions. A learning region is characterized by regional institutions which facilitate individual and organizational learning through the coordination of flexible networks of economic and political units.[25] The *regional network creating the learning region* is not confined to economic units, but also includes social, political and institutional players where the transfer of information and knowledge is a natural and frequent process. According to Jewtuchowicz, in the concept of the learning region, the key is to show in what way the region can get involved in globalization, initiating various processes of learning on the basis of a defined area which is a dynamic and changing system.[26]

The concept of a learning region is based in a particular way on the assumptions of dynamic models of the interactive process of innovation. The process approach to innovation grew on the basis of criticism regarding the traditional linear model of innovation "pushed through" by science or "pulled along" by the market. Innovations are understood as an interactive process emerging between firms and the scientific infrastructure, while also between producers and users at the inter-organizational level and between firms and the wider institutional environment. Therefore, the process of innovation should be seen as an interactive process of learning, in which a large role is played by institutional mechanisms.[27]

The basic attribute of a learning region can be acknowledged as the *regional innovative network* which is a successful mechanism of collective learning and

[23]Keeble and Wilkinson (1999, p. 303).

[24]Florida (2000); Grosse (2002, p. 31).

[25]*Cities and Regions in the New Learning Economy* (2001, p. 24).

[26]Jewtuchowicz (2005, p. 139).

[27]Lundvall (1992); Morgan (1997, p. 493).

generation of innovation. The networks constitute the main source of learning.[28] According to the accepted interactive model of innovation, the processes of innovation in the region take place through networking rather than within the framework of hierarchical structures and markets. Therefore, for the realization of the concept of a learning region, as in the case of the systems of innovation and clusters, key significance is given to the regional dimension of the phenomenon of networking.

Innovation networks concentrate formally independent organizations within the framework of long term relations, bringing with them an exchange of information, an interactive process of learning and direct interaction. In economic categories these networks can be defined as "constellations" of untraded interdependencies, as well as "constellations" of social relations. The network forms of management are preferred to markets and hierarchical structures as they provide more flexibility and are a more long lasting and effective base for the coordination of joint action which can not be found in the invisible market relations.[29] It is worth paying attention to the fact that despite the justified link and similarity between innovative networks and the innovative environment, the afore-mentioned concepts should be differentiated. The innovative network is the organizational arrangement of cooperation and exchange which is established with the aim of the development of knowledge, goods and services. However, the innovative environment is the existing ability of a region in a more institutionalized dimension which leads to the development of innovative networks.[30]

B. Lundvall and S. Borrás in undertaking the problematics of the innovative networks clearly indicate the significant meaning of the defined social norms in the process of networking. In the opinion of the authors, innovative networks can only develop in the presence of the required minimum level of mutual trust. As a consequence, it is acknowledged that innovative networks are always socially conditioned. Networks work best as innovative social systems in a situation where various areas of tacit knowledge of a regional nature are used such as the following: association, enterprise and the organization of the business environment. This occurs because the exchange of tacit knowledge requires greater trust and cultural understanding which is developed thanks to geographical proximity.[31]

This is also why according to P. Cooke, the catalysts of innovative networks should be non-profit type organizations, as they usually enjoy the most trust. Organizations such as for example, agencies of regional development are to fulfil the function of a regional animator responsible for facilitating interactive processes between enterprises and the R&D area.[32] This is confirmed by the justification of the accepted claim of the important role of social capital and non-economic interdependencies in the coordination of procedures in the regional economy.

---

[28]Okoń-Horodyńska (2000, p. 18).

[29]Lundvall and Borrás (1997, p. 105).

[30]Lundvall and Borrás (1997, p. 107).

[31]Lundvall and Borrás (1997, p. 106).

[32]Cooke (1996, p. 166).

Innovative networks take on a more or less formal nature and are identified by the organizational structures which are focused on the generation of innovation. It is possible to distinguish categories of innovative networks based on more formalized agreements on cooperation such as *joint ventures* that are regulated by agreements referring to as jointly realized R&D work or trading agreements regarding the exchange of the results of research work. Innovation networks also arise from the financial involvement of enterprises in the form of direct investment or licensing of technology. A lower market dimension is adopted by innovative networks as a result of joint research associations and also networks as an aim of participating in research programmes financed by public funds. Networks that are maintained thanks to an informal exchange of knowledge between enterprises through the means of scientists and engineers who are employed there are of an informal nature.[33]

A particular category of innovative networks is that of institutionalized mechanisms of R&D interaction involving partners of the industrial and scientific sectors. It is possible to add the scientific and technological centres, technological incubators and technology transfer centres. This type of innovative network of interaction is aimed at first and foremost the stimulation of transferring knowledge from the R&D sector to the industrial sector and with relation to this, they provide many mechanisms facilitating the process of transferring and commercializing knowledge.

Using the flows of knowledge in a spatial dimension as a mechanism which stimulates the innovative ability of a region is also emphasized from the perspective of creating effective systems of innovation. The *concept of innovative systems* constitutes a higher level of development in terms of the concept of innovative networks, the learning region, the local innovative environment and clusters. This is to a greater extent based on the theory of systems and the role of social networks in the flow of knowledge and the creation of innovation in the region. The aforementioned terms are attempted to be combined as one presenting it as successive stages in the development of the region in question – from the innovative cluster to the learning region, right up to the highest forms of development in the shape of a regional system of innovation.[34] The learning region is seen as a particularly effective type of regional system of innovation.[35] A regional system of innovation is based on flexible network arrangements which generate the basis for innovativeness in the economy of the region.[36] It is necessary to remember that the idea of a regional system of innovation grew on the basis of the concept of the system of innovation in a wider sphere, defined on a national scale and described as a *national innovation system*.[37]

---

[33]Pyka (2002, p. 161).

[34]Cooke (1997); Olejniczak (2003, p. 66).

[35]*Cities and Regions in the New Learning Economy* (2001, p. 24).

[36]Stawasz et al. (2006, p. 4).

[37]Lundvall (1998).

The concept of *regional systems of innovation* is based in its assumptions on the evolutionary theories of technological changes. K. Morgan justifies the aforementioned theory by distinguishing two fundamental aspects which enable the observation of the relation between the theory of evolutionary economics and the idea of the system of innovations:[38]

- Innovation is an interactive process that occurs between enterprises and scientific infrastructure, between various functions in an enterprise, between producers and users at an inter-organizational level and between enterprises and the wide institutional environment. That is why innovation should be seen as the interactive process of learning in which an important role is to be played by a range of institutional mechanisms
- Innovation is formed by various types of institutional rules and social norms. The idea of an institution is understood in the categories of repetitive behavioral and custom patterns, conventions and routine. All these norms help in the regulation of economic life by reducing uncertainty in activities

On the basis of the aforementioned assumptions a wide concept of the system of innovation has been created taking account of both the dimension of the economic process of innovation, as well as the social nature of this process. From this aspect such a system is interaction and cooperation of various categories of regional interested parties in the process of creating and using knowledge. The necessary condition for the effective functioning of the system is the existence of a well formed social network between all the players taking part in the regional processes of innovation.

As already stated, within the framework of the characteristics of networks of innovation and the concepts of learning regions and also the concept of an innovation system based on the assumption that the interdependencies between the players of the process of innovation have an impact on its dynamism and as a result have an impact on the competitiveness of the given location. This system is dynamic and involves constant evolution and one of the most important factors that influence its development is the ability of learning in the case of particular units and the system itself as a whole. Innovation arising from within the framework of a system is the result of interaction and feedback between the players dealing with creating, transferring and using different types of knowledge.[39] That is why the number of institutions involved in the functioning of the system of innovation and the increasing amount of channels for providing access to external sources of knowledge is essential. In the process of creating and distributing knowledge within the framework of the system such units become involved as: colleges, R&D units, technology transfer centres, technological centres, institutions of the business environment etc. The effectiveness of gaining and using the knowledge of these institutions has an impact on the successes of these enterprises.[40]

---

[38]Morgan (1997, p. 493).

[39]Szultka et al. (2004, p. 7).

[40]Szultka et al. (2004, p. 7).

Therefore, the regional system of innovation should be seen in the categories of cooperating organizations involved in the processes of creating, diffusion and using knowledge and innovation in the region in question. The system of innovation in a regional dimension is a "public and private forum of interaction in the world of business, local and state administration, scientific and research and educational institutions, as well as supra-governmental institutions facilitating the activation of local factors of growth and better use of resources."[41] The system of innovation is the flexible socio-economic arrangement of wide ranging connections, which is capable of using local resources and factors determining the processes of production appropriately to the specifics of the regional market. It is necessary to underline that it is not possible to define one universal model of such a system.

Within the framework of the system of innovation, innovative enterprises enter mutual interactions with their suppliers, clients, as well as competitors in creating at the same time one of the pillars of the system – the sphere of entrepreneurs. Enterprises simultaneously cooperate with the sphere of science and research which is mainly responsible for the creation of new knowledge about market potential. This sphere includes the wide spectrum of R&D institutions and colleges, which are the source of technological services, scientific solutions, as well as advisory services and education. The third pillar of the system of innovation, or in other words, its sub-system creates the institutions of local and regional development which fulfil the functions of its own type of catalyst for the whole system. The institutional base of the system is created by organizations that are not focused on profit and realize the programme of supporting regional entrepreneurship. They support the transfer and commercialization of technological knowledge, create the mechanisms that are friendly towards the formation of new innovative enterprises and can also grant financial aid at an increased risk on behalf of innovative enterprises.

[41] Stawasz et al. (2006).

Chapter 4
Regional Disparities in EU

4.1 Statistic Focus on EU Social–Economic Cohesion

4.1.1 EU – 15 and Pre-Accession Countries

In EU countries the process of decreasing the role of the state in favour of international institutions (this phenomenon occurs despite political difficulties with the ratification of the Lisbon Treaty) is accompanied by an increasingly strong trend towards regionalization. In valuing the significance of the growing position of regions in the EU the decision of the Maastricht Treaty was to open a Committee of Regions whose main task is to represent the interests of local and regional communities on the forum of European institutions. The acknowledgement of regional policies as one of the priority levels of activity in the EU was the result of the ever increasing regional variations. As much as in 1950 the ratio between the poorest and the richest regions of countries which later created the EU amounted to 1:5, while in 1988 this ratio reached 1:10.[1]

The strong impulse indicating the need to level out the inter-regional disproportions took place following the accession of Ireland, Greece, Spain and Portugal into the EU. Simultaneously, the stipulations accepted in the Treaty of Rome did not foresee the realization of a regional policy. It was then assumed that the fundamental elements leading to the equalization of the living standards in EU member countries would be the conditions of free competition and a single market.

It is possible to acknowledge the lack of possibilities for regions to realize tasks in the area of investments in infrastructure and restructuring, concentration of development and on the other hand, the worsening of backwardness in peripheral regions as negative phenomena associated with the lack of an appropriate regional policy. Such a state of affairs favoured the creation of increasing inter-regional differences which strengthened the dynamic growth of urban agglomerations, the

[1] "*Sixieme rapport periodique sur la situation et l'evolution socio-economique des regions* (1998).

DOI 10.1007/978-3-7908-2364-6_4,

Table 4.1 Disparities in the level of development of countries candidates for EU membership in 1999

Country	GDP per capitaEU = 100	GDP per capita in the poorest regions	GDP in the richest regions
Bulgaria	22.3	22.2	23.1
Estonia	37.2	–	–
Hungary	49.0	33.1	72.4
Lithuania	31.0	–	–
Latvia	27.7	–	–
Romania	28.2	21.6	40.3
Slovenia	68.8	–	–
Czech Republic	60.3	51.5	114.7
Slovakia	48.6	39.2	99.4
Cyprus	79.3	–	–
Poland	36.1	26.1	52.7

Source: Self-analysis on the basis of the following: *Sixieme rapport periodique sur la situation et le developpement economique et social des regions de l'UE* (1999); *Unity, solidarity, diversity for Europe, its people and its territory* (2001)

process of depopulation of rural areas, growing unemployment especially among young people in peripheral areas far away from urban centres. This economic and demographic phenomenon clearly made it impossible to bring about social and economic cohesion. The increase in the unfavourable economic phenomena caused the necessity of creating coherent regional policy whose tools in accordance with the Single European Act became the structural funds.[2] There is significant geographical variation in the level of economic development which was significantly increased as a result of the last expansion of the EU.

Table illustrates the level of GDP per capita in 1999 with relation to the average EU level, as results from the set of large disparities occur in the group of candidate countries. The highest level of GDP occurred in Slovenia and Cyprus (68.8% and 79.3% respectively) and is close to the level of four countries (Spain, Ireland, Portugal and Greece) in the period of accession into the EU. The remaining group of countries: Hungary (49%), Czech Republic (60.3%), Slovakia (48.6%) or countries in which GDP oscillated at around 50% of the average level for the EU. The third group includes candidate countries with a level of GDP below 40% such as Poland (36.1%). It is possible to note the significant disparities in the level of development of particular regions. In the case of the richest regions (Prague), they indicated a level of GDP that is higher than the average level, and similarly Bratislava approached the average level (99.4%). Likewise, in the territory of the "old EU members" significant variation of regions has occurred and continues to occur as indicated in Table 4.1 which presents the evolution of GDP per capita in regions of the poorest territories of the EU. It is clearly visible that a large group of regions in the period of accession into the EU had very low levels of GDP with

[2]*Les Action structureles 2000–2006* (1999).

Table 4.2 Growth of GDP in the years of 1988–2000 in four countries of EU cohesion

	Period	Greece	Spain	Ireland	Portugal
Average growth of GDP in percentage form	1988–1998	1.9	2.6	6.4	3.0
	1988–1993	1.2	2.0	4.4	2.6
	1993–1998	2.6	3.1	8.5	3.4
	1998–2000	3.6	3.9	8.7	3.3
GDP per capita, EU 15 = 100	1988	58.3	72.5	63.8	59.2
	1989	59.1	73.1	66.3	59.4
	1990	57.4	74.1	71.1	58.5
	1991	60.1	78.7	74.7	63.8
	1992	61.9	77.0	78.4	64.8
	1993	64.2	78.1	82.5	67.7
	1994	65.2	78.1	90.7	69.5
	1995	66.1	78.4	93.3	70.9
	1996	66.9	79.5	94.1	71.1
	1997	66.0	80.0	103.8	74.3
	1998	66.0	81.1	108.2	75.3
	1999	66.8	82.5	114.0	76.1
	2000	67.3	83.1	118.9	75.3

Source: Self-analysis on the basis of the following: *First progress report on cohesion* (2002); *Unity, solidarity, diversity for Europe, its people and its territory* (2001)

relation to the average level of GDP in the EU as a whole. In particular, the regions of East Germany, Greece, Portugal and Spain fell below this level. Table 4.2 presents the trend of changes in GDP in the years of 1988–1998 and also shows the positive aspects of the gradual levelling off of the disparities of socio-economic growth.

The growth trend of GDP in regions of cohesion towards levelling out the disparities in socio-economic growth is presented in detail in Table 4.2.

Table 4.2 presents the changes of GDP with relation to the EU average in cohesion countries. In all four countries there was a clear growth in the level of economic development in the period at hand with the case of Greece from the level of 58.3% to 67.3% (9%), Spain from 72.5% to 83.1% (10.6%), Portugal from 59.2% to 75.3% (16.1%) and the highest growth in the case of Ireland from 63.8% to 118.9% (55.1%). The aforementioned data results in the fact that Ireland almost doubled its level of GDP with relation to the initial state while the remaining countries increased their level of growth from 9% to 16.1% in the years of 1988–2000.

The level of variation in the economic development of EU regions was very varied and fluctuates from 192% of the average GDP per capita in the region of Hamburg (Germany) to 40% in the region of Guadeloupe (overseas territory of France). Simultaneously, the average GDP per capita in the ten richest regions of the EU amounts to an average of 158% of the average level, while in the ten poorest regions it amounts to an average of 50% of the EU average. The disparities in economic development of EU regions are undergoing evolutionary changes in the direction of the levelling out of the level of GDP. In the case of the three most weakly developed countries of the EU, the income per capita in Portugal, Spain and Greece grew from 68% (in terms of the EU average) in 1988 to 79% in 1999.

A huge problem that conditions the achievement of cohesion between EU regions is the issue of the labour market. The problem of rising unemployment in EU countries appeared at the beginning of the 1970s when in 1970 unemployment in EU countries amounted to over 2%[3] and in 1979 almost 6%. In 1985 unemployment rose to over 10.5% reaching the highest level since The Great Depression in the 1930s. The highest level of 11.2% of unemployment was noted in 1994 which equals over 18.5 million unemployed, or in other words, every eighth professionally active inhabitant of the EU was unemployed.

What is interesting is the fact that the growth of unemployment occurred at the same time as the creation of new work places. In the years 1987–1997 the number of new work places in EU countries grew by 5 million, while the number of people entering the labour market amounted to 7.5 million. A characteristic phenomenon is the significant differences in the level of unemployment between particular countries and regions in the EU. For instance, in 1997 in the region of Andalusia in Spain the rate of unemployment amounted to 32%, while over 50% of young people in this region were without work. In this same period in Luxembourg only 2.5% unemployment was noted

The disparities observed in the level of unemployment between EU countries are even more visible if we carry out analysis at a regional level. In almost all the cohesion regions in the analysed period of between 1988 and 1998 there was a clear growth in the unemployment rate. This trend is particularly evident in the eastern German lands where a growth of between 8.6% and 18.1% was observed in Saxony. Against the background of the regions, Ireland clearly marks itself out where the rate of unemployment fell from 16.3% to 7.9%, as well as some regions of Portugal. Two groups of regions are clearly visible which characterize the varying trends – the first group where there was a significant growth of unemployment constitutes the regions of the eastern lands of Germany, while the second group in which there was a drop in unemployment constitutes Ireland and regions of Portugal.

Aside from the changes in the level of unemployment in EU countries and regions, there is also the phenomenon of changes in the level of employment in particular economic sectors that illustrate the transformation of economic structures. Changes in the number of work places in urbanized areas of the EU in the years 1995–1999 are presented in Table 4.3 below.

In analysing the changes in the structure of employment for urbanized areas in the years 1995–1999, as well as the degree of economic development of particular EU countries it is possible to observe the following trends:

- Large variation of changes in the structure of employment
- Growth of employment in services
- In cohesion countries (Spain, Portugal, Greece, Ireland) there are large changes in the sector of employment which can be associated with the transformation of economic structures

[3]All statistical data are taken from the following: *Sixieme rapport periodique sur la situation et l'evolution socio-economique des regions* (1998).

Table 4.3 Changes in the number of work places in the sector of employment in urbanized areas in the EU in the years 1995–1999

Country	Agriculture	Industry	Services	Total
Belgium	–8.9	–2.7	+1.7	+0.5
Sweden	+2.3	–5.9	–0.9	+
Germany	–3.4	–2.4	+0.4	–0.5
Austria	+4.9	–3.2	+0.4	–0.5
Holland	–2.6	+1.9	+3.1	+2.4
Finland	+1.6	+4.2	+3.6	+3.7
France	–4.4	–0.5	+1.2	+0.8
Denmark	–3.1	–1.3	+1.7	+1.1
Great Britain	0.0	–0.8	+1.8	+1.1
Ireland	+1.0	+4.6	+6.4	+5.9
Italy	–16.4	–0.9	+1.1	+0.1
Spain	+0.4	+3.8	+3.4	+3.5
Greece	–4.7	+0.1	+2.3	+1.6
Portugal	–8.0	–3.7	–6.5	–5.6
Total EU 15	–6.4	–0.8	+1.3	+0.6

Source: Self analysis on the basis of *Unite de l'Europe solidarite des peuples, diversite des rerritoires* (2001)

- In the afore-mentioned countries (Spain, Portugal, Greece, Ireland) with the exception of Portugal, employment in industry and services grew
- The growth of GDP was accompanied by the growth in the number of work places in first and foremost industry and services, with Ireland and Spain noted at 5.9% and 3.5% respectively

4.1.1.1 Enlarged EU

The enlarged EU can be divided into three groups of countries. The group of the most developed countries (current 15 without Spain, Portugal and Greece), the middle group of countries including Spain, Portugal, Greece, as well as Cyprus, Malta, Slovenia and the Czech republic where GDP levels out at 80% of the EU average. A real challenge is the third group of the remaining countries where GDP amounts to approximately 50% of the EU average.

The enlargement of the European Union on 1 May 2004 (and further enlargement to include Bulgaria and Romania) was one of the most spectacular and ambitious undertakings in the history of European integration. The problem and the importance of this challenge were and continue to be associated with diversifying levels of not only socio-economic development but also political and even historical and cultural elements to a certain degree. The process of enlargement was connected with very intense anxieties on the side of the "old Union," as well as those of the "new member countries" and resulted from, among other things, big disparities in the level of the economic development and financial transfers connected with structural funds, while also changes on the labour market (the expected rise of unemployment and migration).[4]

As stated in the Fourth Report on the topic of cohesion: The biggest beneficiaries of the policy of cohesion in the period 1994–2006 – Greece, Spain, Ireland and Portugal achieved as a group impressive results in the area of economic growth. In the years 1995–2005 Greece shortened the distance to the remaining 26 EU countries by increasing its income per capita from 74% of the average for the 27 countries of the EU to 88% in 2005. In this period Spain and Ireland increased their indicators from 91% and 102% respectively to 102% and 145% of the EU average. On the other hand, the economic growth of Portugal has maintained a level that is below the EU average since 1999. In 2005 the GDP per capita of this country amounted to 74% of the average for the 27 countries of the EU. Simultaneously, in the new EU member countries particularly those with a very low GDP per capita, it is possible to observe a greater pace of growth and faster catching up with regard to the other EU countries. In the years 1995–2005 the GDP for the three Baltic states increased almost twofold. Likewise, in Poland, Hungary and Slovakia the indicators of growth exceeded the EU average by more than twice. However, due to the very low initial level of GDP per capita, assuming that the growth continues at the current level it will most probably require over 15 years for Poland, and especially Bulgaria and Romania to achieve 75% of the average level for the 27 countries of the EU.

The aim of the enlargement was to strengthen the EU as a unit in the process of globalization and to ensure the real possibilities of competing on the global market. This aim may have been realized in chief through the strengthening of the internal potential of the EU. The policy of socio-economic cohesion is key to this issue and involves the process of levelling off the disparities in the level of development of particular areas of the EU (regions) and the simultaneous economic growth and strengthening of innovativeness.

Nowadays, it is difficult to univocally state whether enlargement ensures the realization of the main aim, but however, it is possible to make an attempt at an initial assessment particularly from the point of view of changes in the structural variations of EU regions. These variations when taking account of the basic economic indicators are very big and it is sufficient to state that the level of GDP per capita as a percentage of the EU average which includes 27 countries, amounted to 251% in Luxembourg,[5] 32% in Bulgaria and 34% in Romania in 2004.

In EU statistics the value of GDP is most frequently provided as a percentage value with relation to the EU average given as 100%. In the enlarged EU over one-third of the population lives in areas where the level of GDP per capita is lower than 90% of the EU average. However, at the regional level, 10% of the population lives in regions where the average GDP level is approximately 31%, while currently 10%

[4]*Enlargement, two years after: an economic evaluation,* European Economy, European Economy (2006).

[5]EUROSTAT data.

of the poorest regions are characterized by having an average level of 61%.[6] Against the background of the situation in EU countries, new EU member countries indicate significant disparities in economic growth with relation to the EU as a whole.[7]

It is possible to analyze the apparent disparities in economic development in terms of many indicators published by EU institutions. The European Commission as well as departments of the EU administration avail of statistical data coming from the statistical bureau of the EU, *Eurostat*, administer their own sets of data (e.g. the general directives of the EC). Moreover, the European Commission uses reports and special data catalogues that are specially prepared by research institutes or expert teams. The data of *Eurostat* is the most often used set of data about the economy and the sphere of the EU social development (partly available free of charge), while in the case of regional cohesion diversifying the level of the socio-economic development inside the Union, cyclical reports concerning the cohesion are published (I, II, III and last IV from 2007, *rapport sur la cohesion economique et social*).

In the period of the last 10 years of the EU reports published on the issue of cohesion, the framework of data reference was changed as a result of the number of the member countries.

The basic EU cohesion indicators are as follows:

- Population (the amount, the population density, the change in the last few years as a percentage of the average for the EU)
- Economy (including the GDP per capita as a percentage of the average for the EU, change in the last few years as a percentage of the average for the EU, the GDP per capita and structure of employment: agriculture, industry, services and expenditure on R&D)
- The labour market (unemployment according to age, sex, long-term unemployment, in which all data is presented as a percentage of the average for the EU,
- Education (level of education as a percentage of the average for the EU) and the new category connected with the realization of the Lisbon strategy *Economic Lisbon Indicators*[8]

In analysing the cohesion process, the most often used tool is that of GDP per capita of a region (according to the parity of purchasing power) with respect to the average level of GDP for all countries of the EU. In EU we can observe many regions with high indicators (developed territories) and many regions with a low GDP level. The level of variation in the development of EU regions presented on the basis of the last report on the issue of cohesion in 2007 entitled: *Rapport sur la*

---

[6]*Sixieme rapport periodique sur la situation et le developpement economique et social des regions de l'UE*, Luxembourg (1999).

[7]Pachura and Nowicka-Skowron (2007).

[8]*Sixieme rapport perodique sur la situation et le developement economique des region de'UE*, CE (1999).

cohesion economique et social. Disparities in the level of development in comparison to 1999 are constantly maintained and are very visible (Graphs 4.1 and 4.2).

Graph 4.1 above presents the variation of the levels of development between EU regions, where 100% of the average GDP constitutes the average level for all regions of the 27 EU countries, thus including the countries of the last enlargement (EU27 = 100%). In this case, the countries of the last enlargement naturally caused a global decrease of the average level of GDP in all regions of the EU. In the following graph however, EU regions have been presented with regard to the average GDP of regions of the "old EU" or the "EU 15" (EU15 = 100%). In comparing these two graphs (Graphs 4.1 and 4.2) a movement of regions is visible

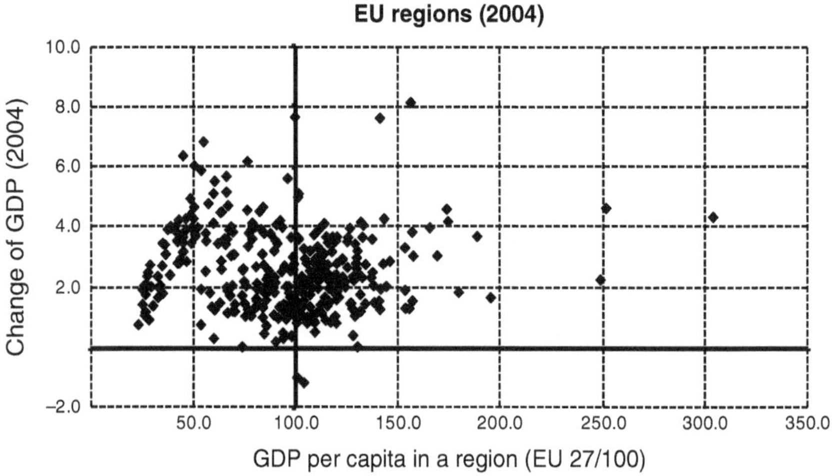

Graph 4.1 EU27 regions (Index EU27 = 100%)

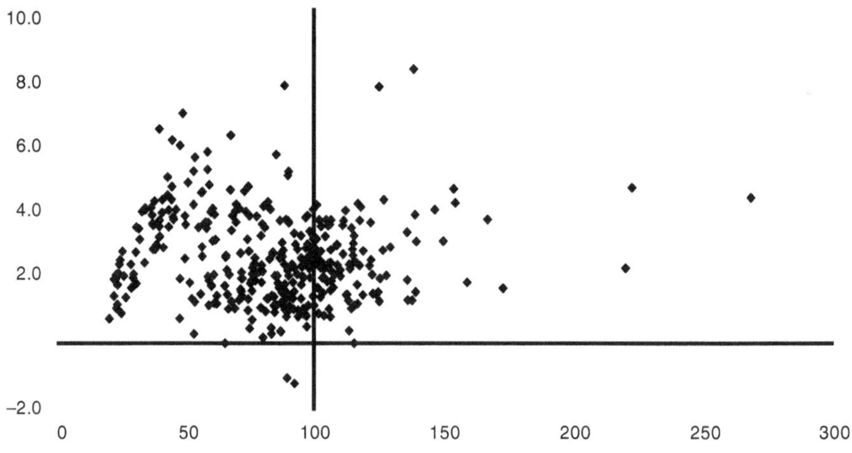

Graph 4.2 EU27 regions (Index EU15 = 100%)

with regard to the vertical axis of the graph constituting a reference point or 100% average GDP level in all EU regions.

On the basis of the data internal variation is also visible in the level of development of particular regions e.g. the average level of GDP for Spain amounts to more than the EU average (100.7%) while the poorest regions of this country namely, Extremadura and Andalusia have a level of GDP at 70%. A similar trend of internal variation is noted in Greece and partly in Portugal. On the map below (Map 4.1) the regional variations of the level of GDP per capita in a region are presented.

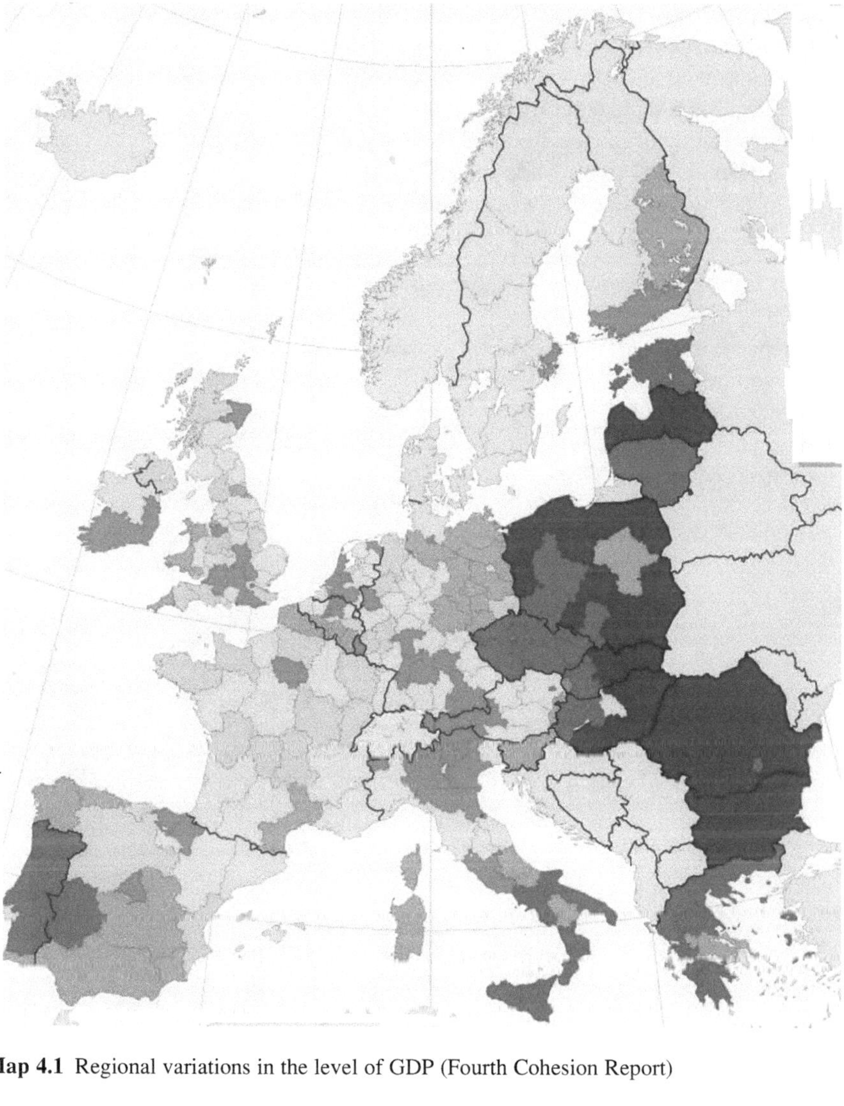

Map 4.1 Regional variations in the level of GDP (Fourth Cohesion Report)

In the new EU member countries of the last two enlargements the phenomenon of internal disproportion in the level of development occurs first and foremost in Poland and Romania (among other reasons, due to the fact of the significantly greater territorial size in comparison with other new cohesion countries). In Poland, the poorest region of Lublin is characterized by an average level of 69% GDP in terms of the country, while in Romania the poorest region is also characterized by an average level of 69% GDP in terms of the country as a whole. In the remaining cohesion countries the internal variation of the level of GDP is characterized by less disproportion in the sustainability of development and as such: in the Czech republic the poorest region has an average level of 77% GDP in terms of the country, while the poorest regions of the following countries amount to the following: Slovakia 76%, Hungary 77%, Bulgaria 77%. The situation of cohesion regions of the new EU member countries is presented in Graph 4.3. This graph presents the level of GDP for regions as well as the average change of GDP in the years 1991–2004.

Another aspect of structural adjustments is the labour market and trends in the area of creating work places, first and foremost due to the significant disparities in the level of unemployment inside the EU itself.

The basic disparities in the structure of employment between the EU and candidate countries involve the following:

- Greater employment in traditional industries despite significant reductions in the 1990s
- Employment in agriculture of approximately 20% is five times higher than the EU average
- Lower productivity with relation to the EU
- Significant growth in employment in the services sector but irregular most of all in urbanized areas

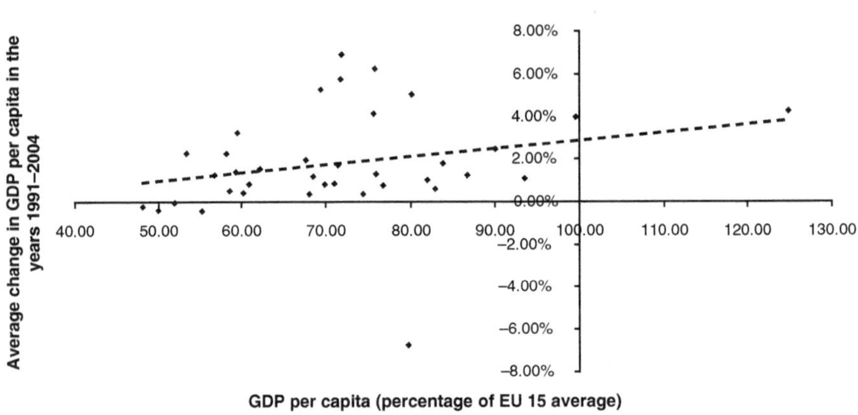

Graph 4.3 Cohesion regions – GDP per capita (EU15 = 100%) in terms of average level of growth of GDP in the years 1991–2004
Source: Self-analysis on the basis of EUROSTAT data

The structure of employment is a very important area of adjustment and is characterized by significant variation. Generally speaking, the least efficient from the point of view of competitiveness is seen to be the structure of employment that is characterized by a significant percentage of the employed in agriculture. However, the dominant form of employment in the services sector is acknowledged to be showing a high level of growth (frequently with the exception of southern European regions that are typically touristic). In the case of the dominating form of employment in industry the situation is not univocal as high levels of employment can indicate an archaic structure where *the traditional decadent industries* dominate, but also indicate the modern and competitive development of the branches of production. Among the regions with a dominating level of employment in services the central regions (capitals) prevail in the particular countries: Brussels, Paris, Vienna, Berlin, Stockholm and traditional regions such as: Ceuta, Provence Cote d'Azure. Simultaneously, it is possible to note that these regions mostly have a higher than average level of GDP. This trend is confirmed by the graph (Graph 4.4) which presents the dependency of the level of employment in the services sector with relation to GDP per capita in a region as a percentage of the EU average as a whole.

A similar trend was observed where the trend of dependency of the degree of industrialization is expressed in the level of employment in industry with relation to the level of economic development as expressed by per capita as a percentage of the EU average as a whole. The most industrialized regions presented mostly have a higher GDP level than the EU average. Saxony clearly differs from these dependencies with only 64% of GDP which is associated with the process of structural adjustments of new German lands and their initial degree of delay in economic development. With relation to Poland, the region of Silesia is characterized by the highest degree of industrialization (45.4% in 1999 and 38.8% in 2004) with

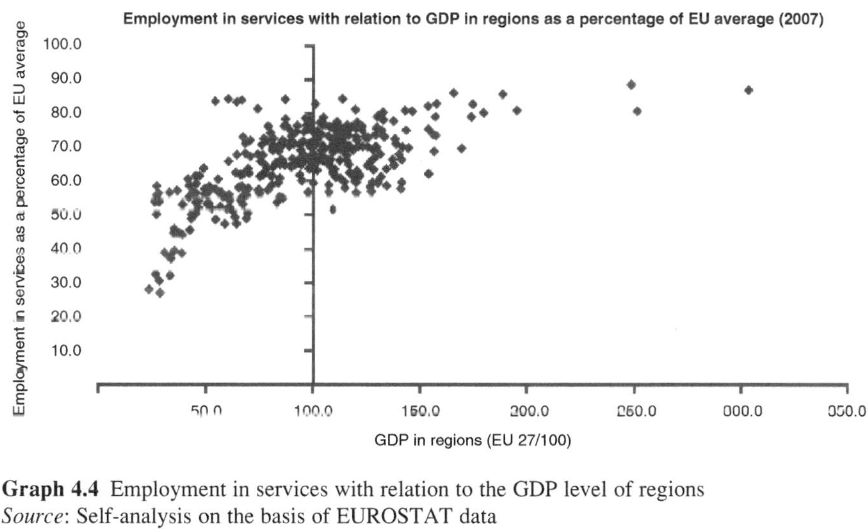

Graph 4.4 Employment in services with relation to the GDP level of regions
Source: Self-analysis on the basis of EUROSTAT data

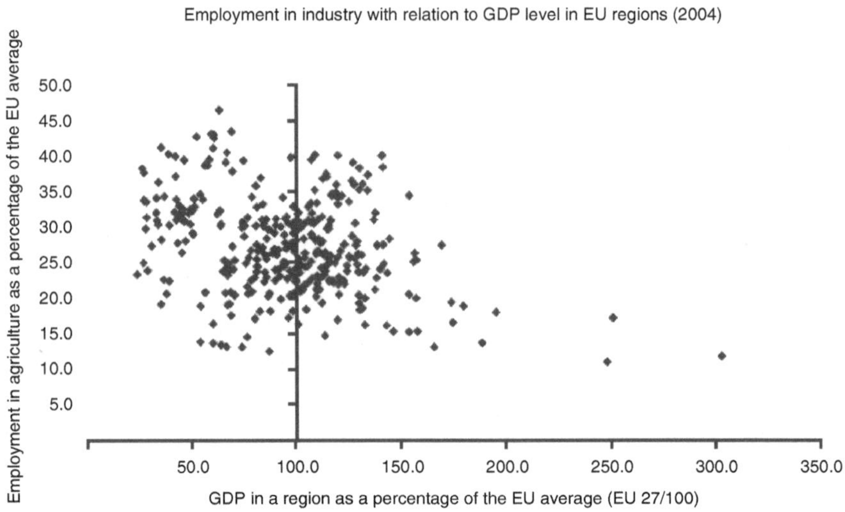

Graph 4.5 Employment in industry with relation to the GDP level in regions (2004)
Source: Self-analysis on the basis of EUROSTAT data

simultaneously a higher level of GDP with relation to the national average (40.3% to 36.1% in 1999 and 57% to 50.7% respectively).

Graph 4.5 presents the EU regions with regard to the level of employment in industry and GDP per capita in the regions. The result from the calculations received facilitated the graphic presentation of regions, which are arranged as in the shape of a district. This is a completely different picture than that received as a result of calculations referring to the level of employment in services. As already mentioned, in the case of employment in services the trend of dependencies of employment in services and the high level of GDP is clearly visible. In the case of employment in industry, it is not possible to notice the dominating trend and univocally point out the dependence between employment in industry and the high level of GDP per capita in the regions.

In the case of agriculture, regions with the dominating level of employment in this branch have clearly a lower level of economic development oscillating at around 60% of the EU average. For instance, in the case of Poland (where one of the highest levels of employment in agriculture occurs) the highest level of employment in agriculture exists in the region of Lublin (35.6% in 1999 and 35.9% in 2004), and simultaneously, the low level of GDP – 26.1% in 1999 and 35.2% in 2004. This confirms the trend of dependence of the structure of employment on the level of economic growth. Regions with the highest level of employment in the services sector and industry have at the same time an above average indicator of GDP per capita. The general trend of development in the labour market in the enlarged EU is to a large degree conditioned by the process of demographic changes. In the EU it is possible to note the process of aging in society which is associated with the drop in the number of people working. A similar situation exists with reference to new EU member countries.

A challenge for the harmony of economic development policy in EU regions is the trend towards the spatial concentration of economic activities in the EU with relation to peripheral areas. There is a large concentration on the central areas incorporating the following: a triangle with the stipulated peaks in North Yorkshire (UK), Franche-Comte (F) and Hamburg (D). This area is one-seventh of the territory of the EU with a population of one-third of that of the EU and a GDP level of almost half of that of the EU (47%). The phenomenon of concentration has negative effects for the peripheral area and also for the centre itself with regard to the impact on the natural environment and social problems. Concentration is associated with large urbanization and an *open economy based on knowledge*. The lack of a *polycentric* structure on the territory of the EU, as well as the high degree of urbanization leads to negative effects in industrial agglomerations. Simultaneously, as stated in the Fourth Report on the issue of cohesion: There is evidence to the fact that the concentration of economic well-being is being reduced in the EU: in 2004 in the traditional economic core of Europe (the area between London, Paris, Milan, Munich and Hamburg) a significantly smaller part of GDP was created in terms of the EU average than in 1995, despite the fact that its share of the population of Europe remained unchanged. This trend should be attributed to the formation of new centres of economic growth such as Dublin, Madrid, Helsinki or Stockholm, but also Warsaw, Prague, Bratislava and Budapest.

4.1.2 Regional Potential of Innovativeness

Comparative analysis in EU regions indicates that the growth of the indicator of R&D in a region (understood as the growth of the number of patents per inhabitant) is directly associated with the growth of GDP. There are of course exceptions connected with the specifics of particular regions.[9] Particular significance in the development of R&D should be given to the case of restructuring of industrial regions. Innovations facilitate the transformation of ineffective economic structures and the creation of work places. Progress in restructuring depends to a great extent on the technological diversification (polarization) of enterprises with relation to traditional sectors.

The significance of R&D in the development of regions and structural transformation is reflected in the functioning of EU policies and in particular the structural funds. In 1994, the European Commission initiated a programme of pilot projects whose aim was to build regional innovative networks.[10] Furthermore, many horizontal programmes exist whose aim is to aid the construction of the networks of diffusion of innovations and relations between research centres and enterprises.

[9]E.g., the Spanish Balearic islands have a weakly developed indicator of innovation in enterprises but a high level of GDP due to the development of the tourism sector.

[10]Article 10 ERDF Innovative actions, EC, Brussels, 2000.

It is necessary to note that the resources from the structural funds are directed to a large extent towards the peripheral regions of the EU which have a weak potential of their own. This policy as aimed at preventing the concentrations of innovations (*cohesion transnational*) particularly in northern European countries. The experience of funds in the period of programming 1989–1993 indicates that the relation between the growth of outlays in the funds in the area of R&D and the growth in the level of innovation and economic growth in the region is not always noticeable. The ability to adapt to new technologies takes on a fundamental importance in the production systems of enterprises, as well as the possibilities of commercialization. In the area of financing R&D there are two inter-regional differences in the requirements of particular regions. In regions with a lower level of development it is necessary to first of all take account of creating the endogen potential. In regions that are in the process of restructuring traditional industries the role of innovation involves the technological diversification in the direction of high technologies and diffusion of innovation with the aim of using the existing potential of human resource.

The fundamental direction of the policies of the EU over the past number of years has become the construction of an economy and society based on knowledge, and in so doing creates its own specific "pressure on innovation." The development of research and innovation was acknowledged as the direct factor of growth in the competence of enterprises and the development of the labour market. The basis of the strategy proposed was univocally defined during the course of the EU summit in Lisbon in 2000.[11]

With the aim of gaining a regional perspective for the Lisbon strategy a synthetic indicator was created known as the Lisbon indicator (Map 4.2). Despite the fact that its destined use is only to gain a general idea of the efficiency of regions within the framework of the Lisbon strategy, nevertheless a region that gains a high rating is on the right way to achieving a range of aims from the Lisbon strategy while a region with a low result is far behind with relation to this.

Regions with an exceptionally high results include regions of Denmark, most regions of Sweden, Etelä-Suomi in Finland (region including Helsinki), regions in south-eastern parts of the UK, Noord-Holland and Bayern in Germany. Regions with the lowest results are located in Romania, Poland and Slovakia where they reflect the simultaneous presence of low productivity, low level of employment and low outlays on R&D. Of the new EU member countries, Cyprus, Estonia, Lithuania, Slovenia and most regions of the Czech Republic gained a rating of above the EU average. In the regions of Slovakia and Hungary which are to be found near the capital cities, they achieved an above average rating while the remaining regions of these countries achieved a rating which was below average and in some cases significantly lower. Large disparities also exist between the results of regions in Spain, Italy and Germany and the southern regions of Spain, Italy and eastern Germany which have low results which in turn illustrates the profound economic disproportions in these countries, as well as the weight of the regional dimension for

[11] *Unity, solidarity, diversity for Europe, its people and its territory* (2001).

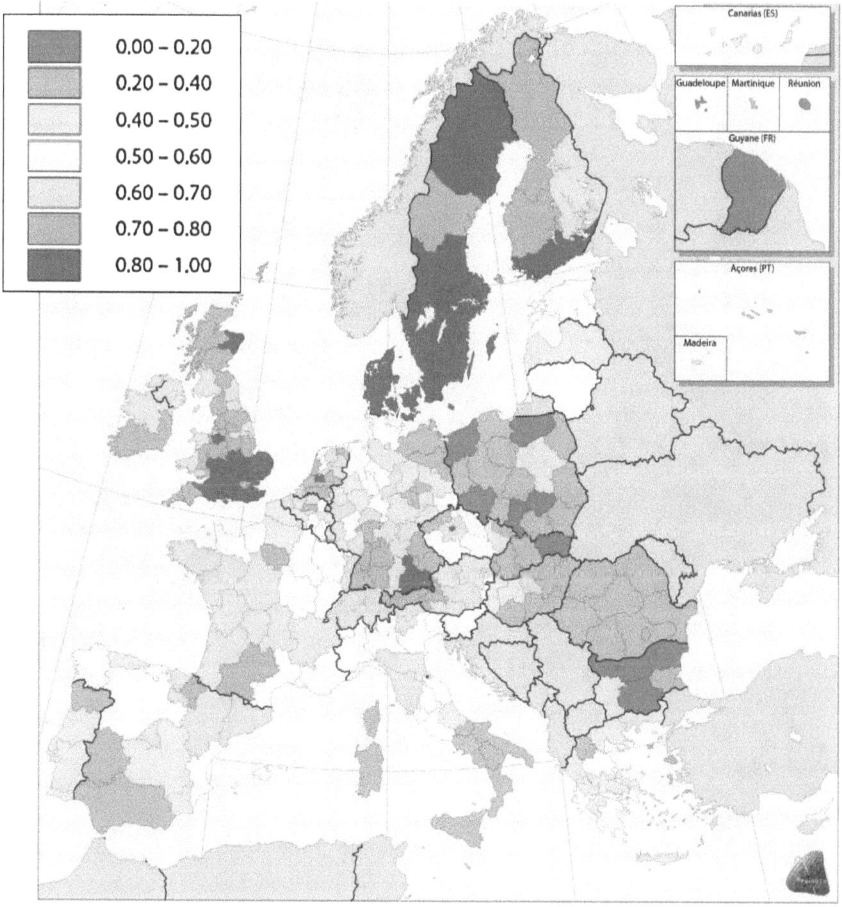

Map 4.2 Lisbon indicators (Fourth Report on economic and social cohesion, the European Commission, 2007)

the Lisbon strategy. Practically all regions that achieved a result below the aforementioned synthetic indicator of the EU average have a level of GDP per capita that is lower than 75% of the EU average, which indicates the weight of the policy of cohesion and the financial support granted within its framework with the aim of facilitating the achievement of the aims of the Lisbon strategy.

As stated in the Fourth Report on the issue of cohesion: EU policy in the area of R&D was in general designed and initiated with the aid of successive framework programmes (FP), which received growing financial support from the moment of their creation in the 1980s. Up to 2013 it is planned that this aid will amount to almost 9 billion Euros which amounts to 75% more than the amount granted in the last year of the previous period of programming in the years of 2002–2006. The projects in the area of R&D laid out by international teams of scientists are selected at the EU level according to the notions agreed at the beginning of the period of

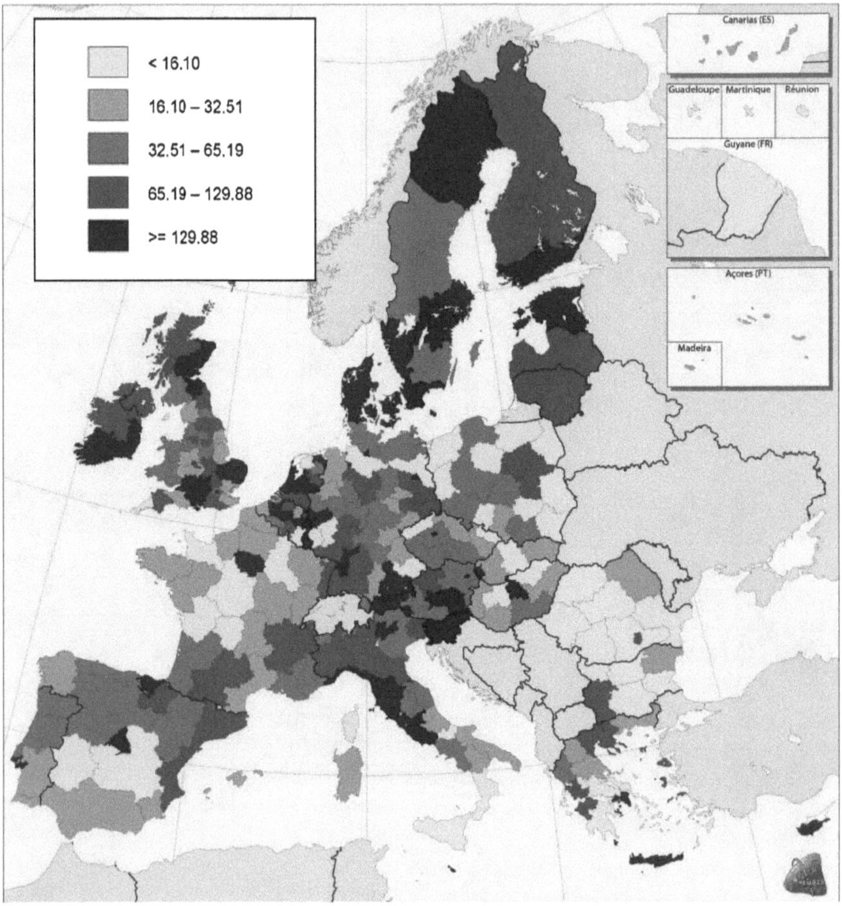

Map 4.3 Regional variations in the participation of the Sixth Framework Programme (Fourth Report on economic and social cohesion, the European Commission, 2007)

programming. The distribution of activity in the area of participation in the Sixth Framework Programme is presented in Map 4.3.

The regional dimension was not to a large extent taken into account in the planning and implementation of the first framework programmes. As a result, despite the fact that the participation of organizations in the cohesion regions increased, it amounted to only 18% of the total participation in the Sixth Framework Programme realized in the years of 2002–2006. The participation in the projects is closely associated with the strong regional and local points and the pattern of the participation constitutes to a large extent the expression of geographical location or concentration, research infrastructure, higher level colleges and to a lesser extent it also explains to the enterprises why in cohesion countries the main beneficiaries of aid from framework programmes are usually capital cities or regions that are well developed from the point of view of economic issues.

Chapter 5
Regional Clustering Based on Efficiency and Networking Models

Among the attempts to assess and classify regions from the point of view of socio-economic coherence, a varied spectrum of criteria and variables is used. In the analysis carried out for the purposes of this dissertation an attempt has been made to classify and analyse the EU regions (NUTS 2) in two fundamental stages:

Stages of research procedure

Stage of research	Activity	Main research tool
I	Recognizing and analysing the varied regions from the point of view of the efficiency of using resources	Data Envelopment Analysis
Ia	Accepting and calculating the "DEA index" indicator constituting the average efficiency of a region	
II	Clustering of regions according to the criteria of efficiency as well as the criteria of "networking"	K-means clustering
IIb	Verification of the results gained	Self organizing map

The main aim of this research is to strive to identify the dependence between the efficiency and adjustment to the initiation of network structures and the achieved results on a macro-economic scale. The variation of the regions from the point of view of efficiency in using resources is aimed at first and foremost, the identification of possible results to be achieved, as well as the illustration of the structures of EU regions from the aspect of efficiency.

With relation to this fact, in the research carried out a measurement of efficiency was decided upon in chosen areas in which the appropriate tool for measuring was chosen for various aspects of efficiency on the basis of technology bordering on data analysis of analytical models. The *Data Envelopment Analysis* (DEA) is a method which serves to assess the productivity and efficiency in cases when we are faced with many categories of inputs and effects. In the second stage of research, the method of modelling based on *K-means* was applied, as well as the method of the *Self Organizing Map* as verification.

P. Pachura, *Regional Cohesion*, Contributions to Economics,
DOI 10.1007/978-3-7908-2364-6_5,

5.1 Models of EU Regional Efficiency

5.1.1 Methodology of the Research Based on Data Envelopment Analysis (DEA)

The non-parametric DEA method was worked out by Charnes, Cooper and Rhode.[1] They applied mathematical programming for the estimation of the level of technical efficiency and created the first known model of *CCR* in literature, which originated from the first letters of the authors of this method. The authors of the DEA method in basing on the concept of productivity formulated by Debreu[2] and Farrell,[3] in defining the measure of efficiency as a single quotient of the effect and single input, used this method for multidimensional situations in which we can have more than one input at our disposal and more than one effect. With the aid of the DEA method the efficiency of the subject matter is measured with relation to other subject matters in the analysed group. In the case of the facilities which lie on the edge of the best practice frontier, their coefficient of efficiency amounts to one. This is a situation where facilities are effective. In the case of facilities lying below the edge of the best practice frontier, the size of the coefficient is less than one and indicates their level of inefficiency.

A simple illustration of the results of the DEA method is presented in Fig. 5.1.

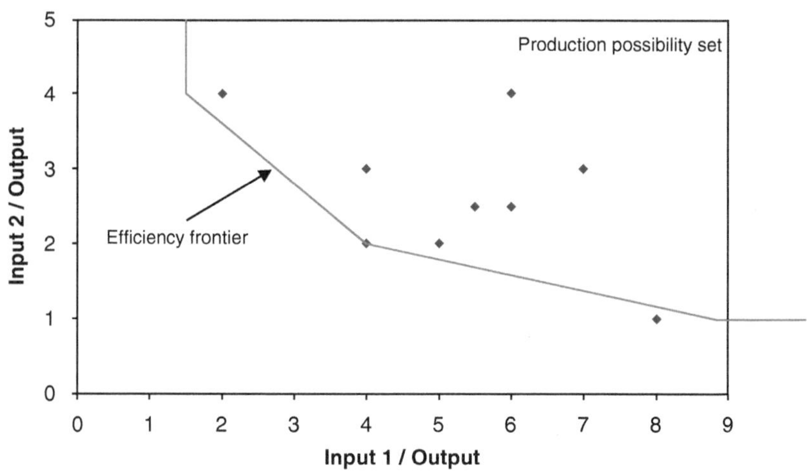

Fig. 5.1 Production possibility set and efficiency frontier for two inputs and one output
Source: Cooper et al. 2001, p. 7

[1]Charnes et al. (1994).

[2]Debreu (1951).

[3]Farell (1956).

A hypothetical set of decision units uses two inputs for the production of one effect. The limits of efficiency are marked out by the units which use the lowest amount of inputs for the production of a specified amount of effects. All units which were not found at the best practice frontier can achieve this by reducing the amount of inputs used. The results of particular DMU, acquired by solutions to relevant problems of linear programming defining their distance from the efficiency frontier.

The measure of technical efficiency in the DEA method is deemed to be that offered by Debreu-Farrell, whose primary definition defines it as the difference between level 1 and the maximum possible reduction of inputs which is technologically possible in the specified amount of inputs (see Fried[4]). Such a defined efficiency takes the value of the range of (0,1). Further modifications of the classic DEA model facilitated the reorientation of it as effects, for which the resultant indicators of efficiency indicate the technically possible increase in the level of effects by using the specified amount of inputs. Such a defined indicator of efficiency takes a value of a range of $(1,\infty)$, where 1 means complete efficiency and a result of over 1 indicates a scale of inefficiency.

Banker[5] proposed developing the model by assuming the constant return-to-scale (CRS DEA) to the model by assuming the variable return-to-scale (VRS DEA). This model in associated literature is marked as BCC, as in the case of the previous abbreviation it is derived from the surnames of the authors (Banker, Charnes and Cooper). This model does not however identify the effects of scale and only Färe[6] modified the BCC model with additional assumptions referring to convexity, which led to the formation of the model of the non-increasing return-to-scale (NIRS DEA). In this analysis the models of VRS were used focusing on the effects in the same form as presented by Cooper.[7]

In the applied approach in the construction of the DEA model, it is not required for the user to write down the weight for each type of input and effect as in the case of traditional index methods. This approach does not require the assignment of a function for a given phenomenon which is usually essential when using statistical and econometric functions of regression.

The DEA method uses the mathematical technique of linear programming, which is able to handle large amounts of variables and relations between them. What is more, the methodology proposed by the DEA method facilitates the analysis of inputs and effects expressed in unrestricted units. This is of particular significance in the case of the assessment of efficiency in the area of intellectual capital whose particular elements are expressed in varied units.

[4]Fried et al. (1993).

[5]Banker et al. (1984).

[6]Fare et al. (1985).

[7]Cooper et al. (2001).

In the DEA method, the subject matter for analysis is the so-called *Decision Making Units* (*DMU*). The subject of the analysis is the efficiency of which a given DMU transforms its own inputs into results. The definition of a DMU is not precise which facilitates flexibility in the use of these methods for various aims.[8] Generally speaking, a DMU is characterized by a separate organizational unit that is responsible for the transformation of specified inputs into the desired effects and whose process is the subject of this analysis. It is important that the DMU under analysis possesses an identical structure of inputs and effects. Such a definition of a DMU facilitates the carrying out of an analysis even with regard to such complicated units as *regions*.[9]

Supposing that there are n DMU: DMU_1, DMU_2, ..., DMU_n. Some common input and output items for each of these $j = 1, \ldots, n$ DMUs are selected as follows[10]:

1. Numerical data is available for each input and output, with the data assumed to be positive[11] for all DMUs
2. The items (inputs, outputs and choice of DMUs) should reflect an analyst's or a manager's interest in the components that will enter into the relative efficiency evaluations of the DMUs
3. In principle, smaller input amounts are preferable and larger output amounts are preferable so the efficiency scores should reflect these principles
4. The measurement units of the different inputs and outputs need not be congruent

One of the first and basic models introduced within the DAE framework is the CCR[12] model, which was initially proposed by A. Charnes, W. Cooper and E. Rhodes[13] in 1978. Let us assume that the number of DMUs has provided data on their inputs and outputs of the production process. In this case, for each DMU one can form the virtual input and output by (yet unknown) weights (v_i) and (u_r):

$$\begin{aligned} \text{Virtual input} &= v_1 x_{1o} + \ldots + v_{\mathrm{m}} x_{mo} \\ \text{Virtual output} &= u_1 y_{1o} + \ldots + u_s y_{so} \end{aligned}$$

Then to determine the weights one can use linear programming so as to maximize the following ratio:

---

[8]Cooper et al. (2001, p. 22).

[9]Complicated in the sense of the complex proces of processing inputs into effects, as well as the interdependencies between them.

[10]Cooper et al. (2001, p. 22).

[11]Although models exist which can also be applied with regard to negative values of inputs or effects.

[12]Also denoted as basic constant return-to-scale (CRS) model in recent literature, see Coelli et al. (2001).

[13]Charnes et al. (1978).

$$\frac{\textit{virtual output}}{\textit{virtual input}}$$

The optimal weights may (and generally will) vary from one DMU to another. Thus, the "weights" in DEA are derived from the data instead of being fixed in advance, and each DMU is assigned the best set of weights.

Suppose m input items and s output items are selected with the properties noted in 1 and 2. Let the input and output data for DMU_j be $(x_{1j}, x_{2j}, \ldots, x_{mj})$ and $(y_{1j}, y_{2j}, \ldots, y_{sj})$, respectively. The input data matrix X and the output data matrix Y can be arranged as follows,

$$X = \begin{pmatrix} x_{11} & x_{12} & \ldots & x_{1n} \\ x_{21} & x_{22} & \ldots & x_{2n} \\ \vdots & \vdots & \vdots & \vdots \\ x_{m1} & x_{m2} & \ldots & x_{mn} \end{pmatrix} \tag{5.1}$$

$$Y = \begin{pmatrix} y_{11} & y_{12} & \ldots & y_{1n} \\ y_{21} & y_{22} & \ldots & y_{2n} \\ \cdot & \cdot & \ldots & \cdot \\ \cdot & \cdot & \ldots & \cdot \\ y_{s1} & y_{s2} & \ldots & y_{sn} \end{pmatrix} \tag{5.2}$$

where X is an $(m \times n)$ matrix and Y is $(s \times n)$ matrix.

Given the data, one can measure the efficiency of each DMU once and hence need n optimizations, one for each DMU_j to be evaluated.. Let the DMU_j be evaluated on any trial and designated as DMU_o where o ranges over $1, 2, \ldots, n$. To obtain the values for the input "weights" (v_i) $(i = 1, \ldots, m)$ and the output "weights" (u_r) $(r = 1, \ldots, s)$ as variables one needs to solve the following fractional programming problem:

$$(FP_o)\ \max\ \theta = \frac{u_1 y_{1o} + u_2 y_{2o} + \ldots + u_s y_{so}}{v_1 x_{1o} + v_2 x_{2o} + \ldots + v_m x_{mo}} \tag{5.3}$$

$$\textit{subject to}\ \ \frac{u_1 y_{1j} + u_2 y_{2j} + \ldots + u_s y_{sj}}{v_1 x_{1j} + v_2 x_{2j} + \ldots + v_m x_{mj}} \leq 1\ (j = 1, \ldots, n) \tag{5.4}$$

$$v_1, v_2, \ldots, v_m \geq 0 \tag{5.5}$$

$$u_1, u_2, \ldots, u_s \geq 0 \tag{5.6}$$

The constraints mean that the ratio of *virtual output vs. virtual input* should not exceed 1 for every DMU. The objective is to obtain weights (v_i) and (u_r) that maximize the ratio of DMU_o, the DMU being evaluated. By virtue of the constraints, the optimal objective value θ^* is at most equal to 1. Mathematically speaking, the non-negativity constraint (5.5) is not sufficient for the fractional terms in (5.4) to have a definite value. This assumption is not treated here in explicit mathematical form. Instead, it is put in managerial terms by assuming that all outputs and inputs have some non-zero value and this is to be reflected in the weights v_i and u_r being assigned with some positive value.

The next step is to replace the above fractional programme (FP_o) by the following linear programme (LP_o),[14]

$$(LP_o)\ \max\ \theta = \mu_1 y_{1o} + \mu_2 y_{2o} + \ldots + \mu_s y_{so} \tag{5.7}$$

s.t.

$$v_1 x_{1o} + v_2 x_{2o} + \ldots + v_m x_{mo} = 1 \tag{5.8}$$

$$\mu_1 y_{1j} + \ldots + \mu_s y_{sj} \leq v_1 x_{1j} + \ldots + v_m x_{mj} \quad (j = 1, \ldots, n) \tag{5.9}$$

$$v_1, v_2, \ldots, v_m \geq 0 \tag{5.10}$$

$$\mu_1, \mu_2, \ldots, \mu_s \geq 0 \tag{5.11}$$

It is important to mention that the measures of efficiency presented here are "units invariant" – i.e., they are independent of the units of measurement used. The optimal values of max $\theta = \theta^*$ in (5.3) and (5.7) are independent of the units in which the inputs and outputs are measured provided these units are the same for every DMU.

Given that this (LP_o) can be solved by the simple method of linear programming, the optimal solution can be more easily obtained by dealing with the dual side of (LP_o), which will be introduced later in this chapter.

In any case let us suppose that we have an optimal solution of (LP_o) which is represented by (θ^*, μ^*, v^*) where v^* and μ^* are values with constraints given in (5.10) and (5.11). We can define the CCR-efficiency as follows: DMU_o is CCR-efficient if $\theta^* = 1$ and there exists at least one optimal (v^*, μ^*) with $v^* > 0$ and $\mu^* > 0$. Thus, CCR-inefficiency means that either (*i*) $\theta^* < 1$ or (*ii*) $\theta^* = 1$ and at least one element of (v^*, μ^*) is zero for every optimal solution of (LP_o).

Let us observe the case where DMU_o has $\theta^* < 1$ (CCR-inefficient). Then there must be at least one constraint (or DMU) in (4.10) for which the weight (v^*, μ^*) produces equality between the left and right hand sides since, otherwise, θ^* could be enlarged. Let the set of such $j \in \{1, \ldots, n\}$ be as follows:

[14]The proof of the equivalency between the fractional programme (FP_o) and the linear programme (LP_o) can be found in Cooper et al. (2001, p. 24).

$$E'_o = \left\{ j : \sum_{r=1}^{s} \mu_r^* y_{rj} = \sum_{i=1}^{m} v_i^* x_{ij} \right\} \tag{5.12}$$

The subset E_o of E'_o, composed of CCR-efficient DMUs, is called the *reference set* or the *peer group* to the DMU_o. It is the existence of this collection of efficient DMUs that forces the DMU_o to be inefficient. The set spanned by E_o is called the efficient frontier of DMU_o.

The (v^*, u^*) obtained as an optimal solution for (LP_o) results in a set of optimal weights for the DMU_o. The ratio scale is evaluated by:

$$\theta^* = \frac{\sum_{r=1}^{s} u_r^* y_{ro}}{\sum_{i=1}^{m} v_i^* x_{io}} \tag{5.13}$$

From (5.8), the denominator is 1 and hence:

$$\theta^* = \sum_{r=1}^{s} u_r^* y_{ro} \tag{5.14}$$

As mentioned earlier, (v^*, u^*) are the set of most favourable weights for the DMU_o in the sense of maximizing the ratio scale. v_i^* is the optimal weight for the input item i and its magnitude expresses how highly the item is evaluated in relative terms. Similarly, u_r^* does the same for the output item r. Furthermore, if we examine each item $v_i^* x_{io}$ in the virtual input

$$\sum_{i=1}^{m} v_i^* x_{io} (= 1), \tag{5.15}$$

then we can see the relative importance of each item with reference to the value of each $v_i^* x_{io}$. The same situation holds for$u_r^* y_{ro}$ where u_r^* provides a measure of the relative contribution of y_{ro} to the overall value of θ^*. These values not only show which items contribute to the evaluation of DMU_o, but also to what extent they do so.

The positive data assumption can be relaxed or rather replaced by semi-positive data assumption. All data is assumed to be non-negative but at least one component of every input and output vector is positive. It can be referred to as semi-positive with mathematical characterization given by $x_j \geq 0$, $x_j \neq 0$ and $y_j \geq 0$, $y_j \neq 0$ for $j = 1, \ldots, n$. Therefore, each DMU is supposed to have at least one positive value in both input and output. A pair of such a semi-positive input $x \in R^m$ and output $y \in R^s$ shall be called *an activity* and shall be expressed by the notation (x, y). The components of each such vector pair can be regarded as a semi-positive orthant point in $(m + s)$ dimensional linear vector space in which the subscript m and s specify the number of dimensions required to express inputs and outputs, respectively. The set of feasible activities is called *the production possibility set* and is denoted by P, and it has the following properties[15]:

1. The observed activities (x_j, y_j) $(j = 1, \ldots, n)$ belong to P
2. If an activity (x, y) belongs to P, any semi-positive activity (tx, ty) belongs to P for any positive scalar t. This property is called *constant returns-to-scale* assumption.
3. For an activity (x, y) in P, any semi-positive activity $(\bar{x}, \bar{y})$ with $\bar{x} \geq x$ and $\bar{y} \leq y$ is included in P. That is, any activity with an input of no less than x in any component and with an output no greater than y in any component is feasible
4. Any semi-positive linear combination of activities in P belongs to P

By arranging the data sets in matrices $X = (x_j)$ and $Y = (y_j)$, we can define the production possibility set P satisfying (1) through (4) by

$$P = \{(x, y) | x \geq X\lambda, y \leq Y\lambda, \lambda \geq 0\} \quad (5.16)$$

where λ is a semi-positive vector in R^n. So P is the smallest possible set, containing all the activities observed and meeting all the above criteria.[16]

Based on the matrix (X,Y), the CCR model can be formulated as follows:

$$(LP_o) \max \ uy_o \quad (5.17)$$

s.t.

$$vx_o = 1 \quad (5.18)$$

$$-vX + uY \leq \mathbf{0} \quad (5.19)$$

$$v \geq \mathbf{0}, \ u \geq \mathbf{0} \quad (5.20)$$

This is the same as (5.7–5.11), (LP_o) above, which is now expressed in a vector-matrix notation. The dual problem of (LP_o) is expressed with the real variable θ and a non-negative vector $\lambda = (\lambda_1, \ldots, \lambda_n)^T$ of variables as follows:

$$(DLP_o) \min \theta \quad (5.21)$$

s.t.

$$\theta \mathbf{x}_o - X\lambda \geq \mathbf{0} \quad (5.22)$$

$$Y\lambda \geq y_o \quad (5.23)$$

[15]Cooper et al. (2001, p. 43).

[16]Weyman-Jones (2003, p. 43).

$$\lambda \geq \mathbf{0} \tag{5.24}$$

Correspondences between the primal (LP_o) and the dual (DLP_o) constraints and variables are displayed in table.

Primal and dual correspondences

Constraint	Dual variable	Constraint	Primal variable
(LP_o)	(DLP_o)	(DLP_o)	(LP_o)
$vx_o = 1$	θ	$\theta x_o - X\lambda \geq 0$	$v \geq 0$
$-vX + uY \leq 0$	$\lambda \geq 0$	$Y\lambda \geq y_o$	$u \geq 0$

Source: Cooper (2001, p. 44)

(DLP_o) has a feasible solution $\theta = 1, \lambda_o = 1, \lambda_j = 0\ (j \neq o)$. Hence the optimal θ denoted by θ^*, is not greater than 1. On the other hand, due to the non-zero (i.e., semi-positive) assumption for the data, the constraint (5.24) forces λ to be non-zero because $y_o \geq 0, y_o \neq 0$. Hence, from (5.23), θ must be greater than zero. Putting this all together, we have $0 < \theta^* \leq 1$. The constraints of (DLP_o) require the activity (θx_o, y_o) to belong to P, while the objective seeks the minimum θ that reduces the input vector x_o radially to θx_o while remaining in P. In (DLP_o), we are looking for an activity in P that guarantees at least the output level y_o of DMU$_o$ in all the components while reducing the input vector x_o proportionally (radially) to a value as small as possible.

Under the assumptions of the preceding section, it can be said that ($X\lambda$, $Y\lambda$) outperforms (θx_o, y_o) when $\theta^* < 1$. With regard to this property, we define the input excesses $s^- \in R^m$ and output shortfalls $s^+ \in R^s$ and identify them as "slack" vectors by:

$$s^- = \theta \mathbf{x_o} - X\lambda, s^+ = Y\lambda - y_o \tag{5.25}$$

with $s^- \geq 0$, $s^+ \geq 0$, for any feasible solution (θ, λ) of (DLP_o).

The interpretation of λ vector, being the solution of (DLP_o), is connected to the participation of all DMUs in the evaluation of DMU$_o$. The values of λ indicate, which efficient DMUs and in what proportions participated in the DMU$_o$ evaluation.

5.1.1.1 Introduction of *DEA* Models for Regional Analysis on EU Level

In this book, an attempt has been made to evaluate efficiency at a regional level, while for the DMU particular *regions of the EU* were accepted at the level of NUTS 2. It is possible to debate whether indeed the regions fulfil the fundamental condition of realizing a credible analysis with the aid of the DEA method, or in other words, are they sufficiently congeneric from the point of view of the examined technology. Taking account of the fact that the research was put through efficiency in the transformation of the inputs into effects in an area that is very general without undergoing detailed analysis this process continues with only a set of inputs and effects. This process at a regional level is not described and identified in a sufficient way to be able to defined a closed set of technological possibilities.

With relation to the doubts described above, the following assumptions have been adopted:

1. It was assumed that interdependence exists between the particular inputs and the effects in the form of GDP per capita
2. The analysis was put through the efficiency of transformation of inputs into effects according to the identified interdependence above
3. Models were constructed for the purpose of calculating the fractional indicators of efficiency as only some variables describing the functioning of regions were used in their construction
4. The variables used in the models do not entirely describe the processes analysed

The first assumption is first and foremost connected with the constantly incomplete knowledge in the area of socio-economic processes at a regional level, as well as a large number of factors which has an impact on this process and which can exert this impact. In the research carried out, it was decided to use only those factors which clearly involve interdependence or where it is commonly acknowledged. On the other hand, the research presented is of a cognitive nature and can lead to the identification of similar interdependences which up to now had not been included in research or were not commonly acknowledged.

The second assumption is a direct result of the first assumption, only introducing a measure of efficiency of transforming inputs into effects as the fundamental aim of this work. The introduction of a greater number of factors in the evaluation of efficiency has been consciously rejected, by placing emphasis on the description and analysis of the interdependence indicated in the first assumption. This enables the precise identification of the efficiency of these interdependences without placing them however, in more complex arrangements of inputs and effects.

Finally, the third assumption is associated with the specifics of the DEA method and its sensitivity to the number of attempts and amount of variables used. With relation to the limited number of research attempts (148 regions, for which a complete set of variables was accumulated) the number of variables used in particular models was restricted.

The regions, as analysed DMUs, use significantly more inputs which shape or can shape the level of GDP than that which is portrayed in the analysis. This is similar to the case of the achievement of other effects apart from GDP in this area. The fourth assumption is associated with the fact that in taking account of all these factors, it was not first of all possible, and secondly, it was not the aim of the research carried out. The acceptance of the level of GDP per capita as one effect in the particular models serves to first and foremost unify and simplify the interpretation of the resultant indicators of efficiency (the indicators of efficiency gained facilitate the identification of the lacks in the area of the level of GDP with comparison to the best regions) by narrowing it down to a common denominator (the level of GDP taken into account is calculated in accordance with one inhabitant), as well as including the indicator in a possibly wide category.

In summing up the assumptions, it is necessary to underline that they have the aim of guaranteeing the clarity of the advanced approach for the research task realized. In this area, it is necessary to admit that the methodology used is of an innovatory nature and the aim of its application in current research is also the verification and confirmation of its usefulness. The indicators of efficiency should be treated more as data for categorization than for absolute amounts.

> In the research carried out five models of DEA were used, of which each one describes a chosen aspect of using resources in regions and their transformation into effects is expressed in the form of the most universal indicator which is that of GDP per capita.

5.1.1.2 Construction of DEA Models – Construction and Justification

In the construction of the five models of efficiency, groups of fractional indicators were used which were applied for the calculation of the values of the DEA coefficients. The statistical indicators were applied in a varied sphere, which means that some of them constitute variable inputs or effects in more than one model. This particularly refers to the growth indicator of GDP per capita, which is most frequently used as a variable indicating effects. According to the research procedure, the repetition of indicators and their varied configuration is permissible and at the same time narrows down the final amount of indicators necessary for generating five models. The choice of fractional indicators is justified due to the particular meaning of information which is a conductor, which in effect provides

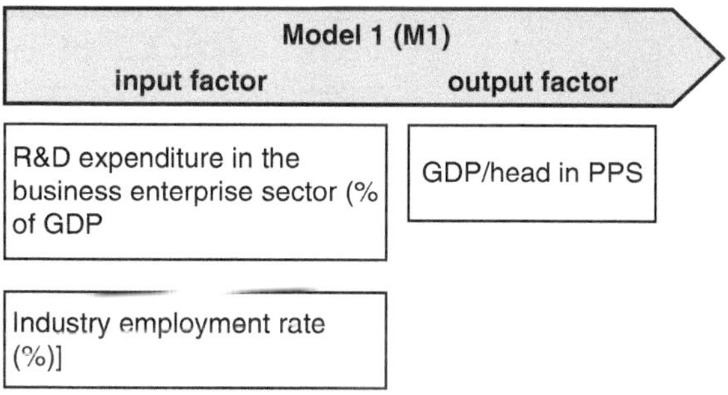

Model 1 (M1) structure

the specified possibilities of interpreting the emerging phenomena in the area of socio-economic coherence of the regions analysed.

One of the most important synthetic indicators in the area of innovativeness or in terms of a more narrow understanding – R&D statistical activity, which constitutes the basis for the processes of innovation and its most creative part. This indicator is counted among the categories of the so-called "arrangement," and a more precise dimension of innovation referring to the creation of knowledge or the sources of innovation. This means that it refers to resources designed for R&D activity. It is possible to view this as an indicator which illustrates the level of investment in R&D activity, or in the creation of new knowledge. This is a key element in the construction of an economy based on knowledge. Expenditure on R&D activity constitutes one of the main factors that drive economic growth in conditions of the knowledge based economy. They are essential for carrying out the transformation in the direction of an economy based on knowledge, as well as for the improvement of production technology and the stimulation of economic growth. With relation to this, the growth trend of value for this indicator over a time scale is the basic sign of competitiveness and prosperity in a region in the future. R&D activity fulfils an essential role in generating innovation and should be seen as a fundamental element in the processes of innovation. This is an activity which by assumption is to lead to the initiation of innovation. However, depending on the type of R&D activity undertaken, it leads to in varying degrees to the generation of innovation. Most frequently, most of the R&D work indicates an association with innovations of a product and process nature and more rarely lead to the creation of organizational and marketing innovations. Simultaneously, all types of research should be acknowledged as a type of activity with an innovative nature, although basic research by nature does not refer to specified or precisely defined innovations in advance. Therefore, expenditure on R&D activities is acknowledged to be that which is incurred for innovative activity, which is to bring specified effects in the form of generating new solutions leading to the reduction of uncertainty in the area of a defined area of knowledge. The strategic aim of the EU is to strive for the achievement of an indicator value at the level of 3% GDP by 2010, while two thirds of the source of financing should be from funds which come from the entrepreneurial sector.

That is why the indicator that takes account of the share of enterprises in the outlay on R&D is used as a reference point in this analysis. The share of economic units in the structure of financing R&D activities should significantly exceed the value of public funds and work out at around 2/3 of the whole structure of financing. The greater the level of expenditure on R&D activities, the more modern the production usually is, or the greater the opportunities of its modernization. This indicator can be seen in the categories of stimulating the commercialization of R&D work, as the financing of this work with the funds of private economic units is going in the direction of initiating market solutions. The high level of the indicator reflects to a large degree the level of financing of applied research leading to practical applications. This results from the fact that in the nature of the functioning of firms these are usually directed towards applied and development research.

As the second indicator of outlays in the model, it enables the illustration of the efficiency of the labour force at the level of industrial branches. A lower indicator value against a high level of GDP per capita in the region shall reflect the high level of labour efficiency and the modern nature of production processes, in which the main role is played by automation of work by using production technology. In connection with the outlays on R&D activities in industry, they are shown in a way of a more complex process of processing the potential of industrial enterprises into economic results.

GDP per capita in PPS is the fundamental indicator of economic statistics that reflects economic results and the level of economic growth in the regions and is used in most socio-economic research in assessing the living standards of inhabitants and the degree of economic development. It is also one of the most frequently applied measurements of the wealth of a region and its inhabitants. Taking account of the number of inhabitants, the actual picture of the economic potential of the region and the growth in living standards of the inhabitants is presented. This indicator is found in most models of DEA within the framework of the category of effects, which facilitates the indication of the efficiency of processing particular categories of resources in terms of economic results and the prosperity of inhabitants.

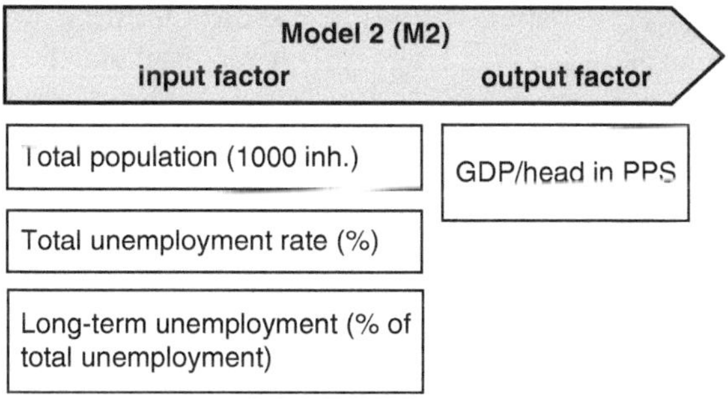

Model 2 (M2) structure

This indicator shows the potential of human resources in the region in a quantitative sense, while fulfilling its role exclusively in connection with the additional indicators, which has been accounted for in the model. In this way, it should be treated as a complementary indicator with relation to the two remaining variables within the framework of inputs which are key to the model. Thanks to this it is possible to portray the impact of the amount of human resources on the economic result of regions with the further involvement of other indicators from the category of inputs. This facilitates the correction of deformation in the interpretation of the efficiency coefficient in the case of regions with a high level of GDP but a large amount of inhabitants.

The total unemployment rate (%) illustrates the increase in the phenomenon of unemployment in a given population by calculating the value of the ratio of the number of people unemployed with the labour resources in the region. The measurement of general efficiency and quality of human capital illustrates the appropriate preparation of human resources for the fulfilment of the functions of the efficient factor of production. It is a symptom of matching the supply of labour to the demand for specified professional qualifications. This allows the illustration of the degree of matching labour resources to the changing economic situation and market changes. This is a general indicator that characterizes the situation of labour resources in the labour market. The interpretation of the indicator however, requires a great deal of care due to the complex problematic of the labour market and the phenomenon of unemployment itself. Thanks to the inclusion of the indicator the marking out of the efficiency of the impact of the phenomenon of unemployment on the level of economic development in the regions becomes possible. A lower value of the DEA indicator means a lower impact of unemployment on economic results, which should be interpreted as a positive occurrence. Despite the high rate of unemployment in the region satisfactory economic results are achieved. At the same time the relation of interdependence between unemployment and the level of economic growth in the regions is portrayed.

The completion of the set of indicators of inputs with the variable of long-term unemployment (percentage of total unemployment) leads to the intensification of the analysis of the processes of social coherence in the regions. Long term unemployment is the most threatening of types of unemployment and not only leads to material degradation but also first and foremost to social exclusion. This indicator can also to a certain degree, be a source of information on the topic of social and citizen activity as the long term unemployed are characterized by a limited degree of this type of activity.

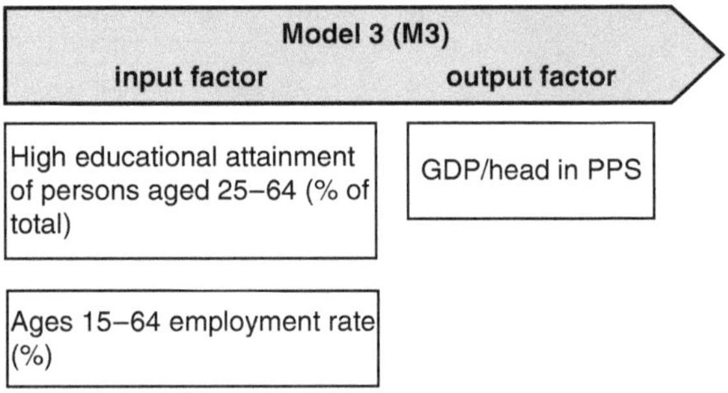

Model 3 (M3) structure

The high level of education attained by people aged 25–64 (as a percentage of the total) is a fundamental indicator illustrating the formal level of education of society and the resulting knowledge resources. Education should be treated here as an investment in knowledge which can assure satisfying remuneration and perspectives of professional development. Highly educated inhabitants of the region are the foundation of development for the knowledge society which is the condition for the realization of the aims of the *Lisbon Strategy*. A high level of education reduces the risk of unemployment and increases social prestige, as together with the increase in education there is a rise in the opportunities of gaining work and higher wages while also the mobility of professional employees rises. A high level of education provides the possibility of professional and social advances and can be viewed as one of the factors counteracting social exclusion. Furthermore, the highly qualified human resources indicate a particular ability to absorb innovation, new solutions and acceptance of the constant occurrence of changes in the socio-economic environment. Thanks to the inclusion of the indicator in this model it is possible to observe the efficiency of the impact of the education of inhabitants on the level of economic growth of the regions.

The indicator of the employment rate for people aged 15–64, reflects the degree of professional activity of the inhabitants. Its low value proves the inappropriate adjustment of professional qualifications, particularly older people to the situation on the labour market. It also shows the participation of people in the creation of economic wealth and on the other hand, unused reserves of human resources, whose use would improve the economic results. Passive labour resources require economic means for consumption and at the same time do not directly lead to the creation of GDP. Within the framework of the model, the indicator slowly shows the efficiency of the impact of professional activity of society on the economic results achieved.

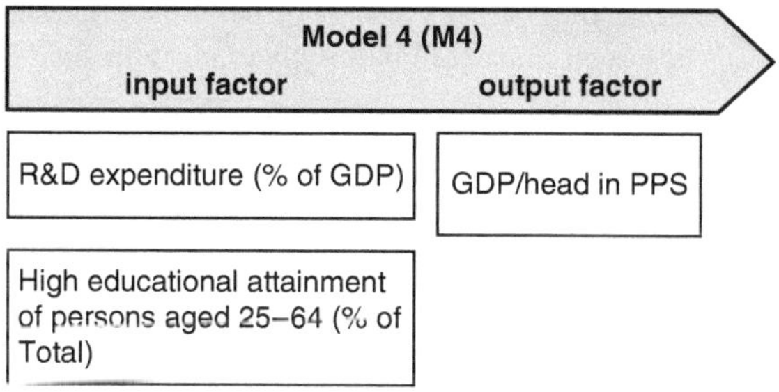

Model 4 (M4) structure

The significance and justification of the indicators used in model 4 have already been defined, in which the first of them refers to the model of inputs on R&D activities and not separate expenditure at the level of the entrepreneurial sector as in model 1. This does not change however the area of justification for this choice. The measured value of expenditure is becoming increased by expenditure on the level of the remaining economic sectors, mainly the expenditure financed by public funds.

In this way, the set of indicators chosen illustrates the general potential of the knowledge resources in the region in question, as well as the ability to create and initiate innovation. This model presents the efficiency of processing these resources in the prosperity of society, which is measured by the value of GDP per capita. The DEA coefficient to a certain extent illustrates the value of GDP in the regions

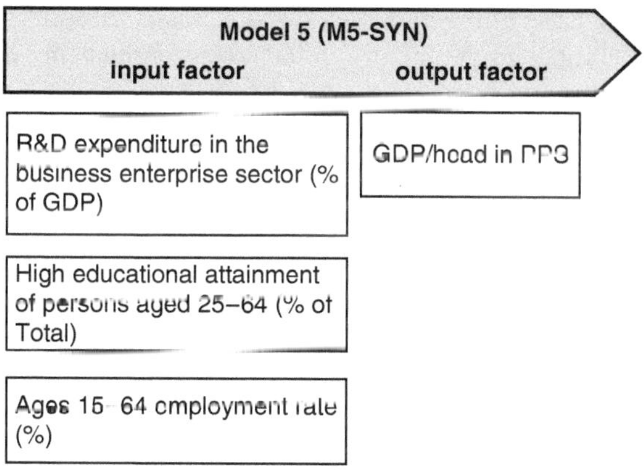

Model 5 (M5-SYN) structure

analysed and is adequate to the inputs incurred in the form of highly educated labour resources and expenditure on R&D activities. Regions shall be shown whose value of GDP should be higher with relation to the inputs incurred against the background of the whole population analysed.

All these fractional indicators have been used in earlier models and were justified according to their use. The configuration of the indicators results from the need to analyse the efficiency of processing knowledge resources (highly educated labour resources + expenditure on R&D) in the dimension of the industrial sector. As opposed to the similar in type indicators in model 4, the model presented here was directed at the industrial sector, which is to show its efficiency in the process of creating GDP in terms of the population analysed. A set of further models has been presented below together with their characteristics (Table 5.1).

5.1.2 Presentation and Interpretation of Research Results

As a consequence of the assumptions of the construction of the analytical models on the basis of DEA methodology the indicators for particular EU regions were calculated. The research constituted regions in the EU at the level of NUTS 2. The research was confined to the regions for which the statistics in the area of the variables used in 2004 and 2005 were accessible. Following the elimination of these regions for which the data referring to at least one of the variables used was inaccessible there was an attempt made at research that included 148 regions. Their specification was presented together with the efficiency indicators achieved in Table 5.2.

As already mentioned above, each of the models applied was oriented on the effects (therefore the results gained indicate the scale of the possible increase of GDP with regard to the inputs applied) and the efficiency indicators were calculated on the basis of the variable effects of scale, assuming at the same time the limited possibilities of the regions in the area of influencing its size.

According to the accepted methodology of measuring efficiency, the efficient regions in a given model achieved the result equal to 1. The aforementioned results above 1 indicate inefficiency in a given model that illustrates the scale of inefficiency. The further away from 1, the more inefficiency in a given model. In order to illustrate the accepted criteria of evaluation the average efficiency indicator was calculated for all the five models. The calculated average should be treated as an indicator that orders the regions according to the efficiency achieved. In the second stage, this average is called the *DEA index* and shall be used for the further categorization of regions (Graph 5.1).

Table 5.1 Characteristics of the DEA models in use

Model	Variable		Interpretation
	Input	Effects	
M1	• R&D expenditure in the business enterprise sector (% of GDP), 2004 • Industry employment rate (%), 2005	GDP/head in PPS (Index, EU27 = 100), 2004	The impact of the indicator of efficiency in the processing of expenditure on R&D in industry, as well as employment in industry on GDP. The main aim of applying the indicator is the differentiation of regions with regard to the significance of industry in terms of GDP for these regions.
M2	• Total population (1,000 inh.), 2004 • Total unemployment rate (%), 2005 • Long-term unemployment (% of total unemployment)	GDP/head in PPS (Index, EU27 = 100), 2004	The efficiency indicator of the impact of long term unemployment and the size of population on GDP. The aim of applying this indicator is the differentiation of regions with regard to the significance of the level of employment and unemployment in terms of GDP for these regions.
M3	• Attainment of high level of education of people aged 25–54 (% of total), 2005 • Ages 15–64 employment rate (%), 2005	GDP/head in PPS (Index, EU27 = 100), 2004	The efficiency indicator of the impact of employment in the working age (15-64), as well as the numbers of graduates on GDP. The aim of the application of this indicator is the differentiation of these regions with regard to the significance of the interactions at the level of education and employment in terms of their GDP.
M4	• Attainment of high level of education of people aged 25-64 (% of total), 2005 • R&D expenditure (% of GDP), 2004	GDP/head in PPS (Index, EU27 = 100), 2004	The efficiency indicator of the impact of expenditure on R&D in total, as well as the numbers of graduates on GDP. The aim of applying this indicator is the differentiation of regions with regard to the significance of the scale of higher level education connected with expenditure on R&D on the level of GDP.
M5 (SYN)	• R&D expenditure in the business enterprise sector (% of GDP), 2004 • Industry employment rate (%), 2005 • Attainment of high level of education of people aged 25–64 (% of total), 2005 • Ages 15–64 employment rate (%), 2005	GDP/head in PPS (Index, EU27 = 100), 2004	The impact of the efficiency indicator of processing expenditure on R&D in industry, as well as employment in industry, size of employment in the working age (15-64), as well as the numbers of graduates on GDP. The aim of applying this indicator is thet synthesization of the previous variables in one model and the significance of their collective impact on GDP.

Table 5.2 Efficiency indicators received in M1–M5 models for particular regions

Region	Symbol	Efectivness factors					*Index DEA*
		M1	M2	M3	M4	M5	M1–M5
Praha	CZ01	12,455	10,629	15,977	15,977	12,455	13,499
Střední Čechy	CZ02	35,928	35,928	18,044	18,044	18,044	25,198
Jihozápad	CZ03	21,478	36,077	18,653	18,653	18,653	22,703
Severozápad	CZ04	21,380	41,365	10,000	10,000	10,000	18,549
Severovýchod	CZ05	29,230	39,435	20,033	20,269	20,033	25,800
Jihovýchod	CZ06	25,262	37,270	22,736	23,283	22,736	26,257
Střední Morava	CZ07	27,635	41,985	22,294	23,775	22,294	27,597
Moravskoslezsko	CZ08	27,925	41,074	18,386	20,985	18,386	25,351
Danmark	DK	20,162	18,437	20,162	20,162	20,162	19,817
Stuttgart	DE11	17,798	17,798	17,798	17,798	17,798	17,798
Karlsruhe	DE12	18,693	18,693	18,521	18,521	18,521	18,590
Freiburg	DE13	21,426	21,901	20,486	20,486	20,486	20,957
Tübingen	DE14	20,882	20,882	20,817	20,817	20,817	20,843
Oberbayern	DE21	14,826	14,826	14,826	14,826	14,826	14,826
Niederbayern	DE22	12,867	21,822	16,586	16,586	12,861	16,144
Oberpfalz	DE23	21,047	21,047	16,321	16,321	16,321	18,211
Oberfranken	DE24	18,272	22,205	17,151	17,151	17,151	18,386
Mittelfranken	DE25	18,298	18,298	16,666	16,666	16,666	17,319
Unterfranken	DE26	20,931	21,395	18,565	18,565	18,565	19,604
Schwaben	DE27	18,530	20,575	17,221	16,172	17,221	17,944
Darmstadt	DE71	15,958	15,958	15,958	15,958	15,958	15,958
Gießen	DE72	18,958	24,182	23,215	23,215	18,958	21,706
Kassel	DE73	14,870	22,282	19,129	14,108	14,863	17,050
Braunschweig	DE91	23,665	23,665	18,581	19,079	18,581	20,714
Hannover	DE92	22,365	22,860	20,470	20,470	20,470	21,327
Lüneburg	DE93	16,426	29,825	21,935	15,237	16,234	19,931
Weser-Ems	DE94	13,980	25,383	18,357	14,520	13,748	17,198
Düsseldorf	DEA1	16,741	19,428	15,432	15,722	15,432	16,551
Köln	DEA2	20,898	20,898	20,489	20,512	20,489	20,657
Münster	DEA3	16,485	26,229	20,100	17,410	16,051	19,255
Detmold	DEA4	18,031	22,999	18,542	17,374	18,022	18,994
Arnsberg	DEA5	17,641	23,676	16,429	17,194	16,429	18,274
Koblenz	DEB1	17,370	26,028	19,543	14,889	17,360	19,038
Trier	DEB2	13,472	26,317	22,674	15,054	13,472	18,198
Rheinhessen-Pfalz	DEB3	23,154	23,154	21,088	21,088	21,088	21,914
Saarland	DEC	13,669	23,182	17,105	16,804	13,107	16,773
Chemnitz	DED1	23,081	30,977	30,977	25,295	22,896	26,645
Dresden	DED2	27,764	27,764	26,962	27,764	26,962	27,443
Leipzig	DED3	19,499	29,218	26,258	28,325	18,660	24,392
Dessau	DEE1	20,820	33,126	27,131	18,949	19,780	23,961
Halle	DEE2	16,415	29,804	22,949	24,337	14,807	21,662
Magdeburg	DEE3	15,723	30,714	29,366	23,203	14,950	22,791
Schleswig-Holstein	DEF	15,159	24,119	19,964	17,483	15,117	18,368
Thüringen	DEG	25,368	30,830	29,419	28,945	24,938	27,900
Eesti	EE	25,582	45,066	45,066	29,665	25,099	34,096
Galicia	ES11	17,323	30,994	28,133	20,141	16,354	22,589
Principado de Asturias	ES12	15,700	28,858	20,391	16,912	13,839	19,140
Cantabria	ES13	12,783	25,602	24,093	13,393	12,065	17,587
País Vasco	ES21	18,000	19,187	20,010	17,031	18,000	18,446

(continued)

Table 5.2 (continued)

Region	Symbol	Efectivness factors					*Index DEA*
		M1	M2	M3	M4	M5	M1–M5
Comunidad Foral de Navarra	ES22	17,590	13,170	19,807	18,588	17,590	17,349
La Rioja	ES23	13,817	14,897	22,949	13,561	13,817	15,808
Aragón	ES24	13,741	17,061	23,372	14,041	13,741	16,391
Castilla y León	ES41	16,623	25,468	25,569	17,772	16,115	20,309
Castilla-La Mancha	ES42	16,028	30,931	24,763	16,309	15,030	20,612
Extremadura	ES43	18,147	37,436	24,485	19,205	1,5,331	22,921
Cataluña	ES51	16,195	18,212	20,841	16,599	16,195	17,608
Comunidad Valenciana	ES52	14,829	24,043	26,248	17,708	14,534	19,472
Illes Balears	ES53	10,000	10,995	17,840	10,000	1,0,000	11,767
Andalucía	ES61	17,455	31,441	22,418	20,150	15,289	21,351
Región de Murcia	ES62	15,775	23,573	26,088	17,513	15,117	19,613
Champagne-Ardenne	FR21	16,037	24,030	18,810	15,215	1,5,518	17,922
Picardie	FR22	21,734	27,723	19,799	20,096	19,799	21,830
Haute-Normandie	FR23	22,342	24,808	18,407	18,550	18,407	20,503
Centre	FR24	21,435	24,875	19,060	19,060	19,060	20,698
Basse-Normandie	FR25	17,765	26,619	21,686	18,482	17,477	20,406
Bourgogne	FR26	18,008	25,498	18,714	17,704	17,826	19,550
Lorraine	FR41	16,997	27,044	20,186	19,604	16,360	20,038
Alsace	FR42	18,259	23,291	22,359	20,443	18,259	20,522
Franche-Comté	FR43	25,705	25,705	18,897	19,300	1,8,897	21,701
Pays de la Loire	FR51	16,343	24,488	20,872	17,002	16,340	19,009
Bretagne	FR52	20,952	25,463	25,307	22,350	20,809	22,976
Poitou-Charentes	FR53	16,758	26,663	21,086	16,883	16,620	19,602
Aquitaine	FR61	21,184	24,584	21,030	21,408	20,861	21,813
Midi-Pyrénées	FR62	25,046	25,046	24,892	24,892	24,892	24,954
Limousin	FR63	17,197	27,362	23,490	17,325	17,196	20,514
Rhône-Alpes	FR71	22,256	22,256	20,750	20,750	20,750	21,352
Auvergne	FR72	26,567	26,567	22,726	22,726	22,726	24,262
Languedoc-Roussillon	FR81	18,438	28,616	20,005	25,447	17,202	21,942
Provence-Alpes-Côte d'Azur	FR82	20,532	23,927	18,442	21,866	18,434	20,640
Corse	FR83	10,000	21,213	13,084	10,000	10,000	12,859
Piemonte	ITC1	18,913	21,000	10,699	11,117	10,699	14,486
Valle d'Aosta/Vallée d'Aoste	ITC2	10,020	10,000	10,000	10,000	10,000	10,004
Liguria	ITC3	15,274	22,887	13,495	14,439	13,119	15,843
Lombardia	ITC4	13,219	15,365	10,018	10,101	10,018	11,744
Veneto	ITD3	10,856	17,731	10,140	10,434	10,140	11,860
Friuli-Venezia Giulia	ITD4	13,438	21,381	11,278	11,844	11,278	13,844
Emilia-Romagna	ITD5	13,598	19,254	11,436	11,436	11,436	13,432
Toscana	ITE1	12,665	21,480	12,427	12,824	12,298	14,339
Umbria	ITE2	12,729	24,865	14,296	15,228	11,978	15,819
Marche	ITE3	12,861	23,352	13,911	14,072	12,470	15,333
Lazio	ITE4	11,522	19,043	11,964	13,127	11,071	13,345
Abruzzo	ITF1	18,593	29,583	16,642	18,845	16,454	20,023
Molise	ITF2	11,304	26,224	15,174	16,630	10,833	16,033
Campania	ITF3	20,213	36,700	10,000	19,089	10,000	19,200
Puglia	ITF4	17,013	35,965	10,000	14,628	10,000	17,521
Basilicata	ITF5	17,041	33,289	11,853	16,719	11,853	18,151
Calabria	ITF6	12,727	36,649	10,591	18,724	10,000	17,738
Sicilia	ITG1	17,946	37,285	10,000	17,754	10,000	18,597

(*continued*)

Table 5.2 (continued)

Region	Symbol	Efectivness factors					*Index DEA*
		M1	M2	M3	M4	M5	M1–M5
Sardegna	ITG2	14,584	30,830	10,000	12,539	10,000	15,591
Kýpros / Kbrs	CY	12,768	25,310	27,472	14,035	12,768	18,471
Latvija	LV	27,976	55,220	44,368	28,212	26,873	36,530
Lietuva	LT	24,429	49,153	47,383	31,123	23,229	35,063
Luxembourg	LU	10,000	10,000	10,000	10,000	10,000	10,000
Közép-Dunántúl	HU21	21,548	41,055	21,371	22,189	19,860	25,205
Nyugat-Dunántúl	HU22	19,237	37,592	21,406	18,967	18,209	23,082
Dél-Dunántúl	HU23	25,389	55,019	25,825	28,143	20,722	31,020
Észak-Magyarország	HU31	28,009	59,072	25,720	24,442	20,931	31,635
Észak-Alföld	HU32	33,164	59,958	27,211	35,612	25,406	36,270
Dél-Alföld	HU33	27,812	56,857	28,376	32,868	23,234	33,829
Malta	MT	20,488	31,160	14,369	18,079	14,369	19,693
Burgenland	AT11	17,082	20,693	16,091	15,350	16,091	17,061
Niederösterreich	AT12	18,190	22,444	17,247	15,913	17,247	18,208
Wien	AT13	13,972	13,972	12,597	12,640	12,597	13,156
Kärnten	AT21	23,111	15,984	15,717	15,717	15,717	17,249
Steiermark	AT22	22,657	18,982	15,827	15,827	15,827	17,824
Oberösterreich	AT31	20,876	17,381	13,748	13,748	13,748	15,900
Salzburg	AT32	11,599	10,000	13,512	12,271	11,592	11,795
Tirol	AT33	16,186	10,000	12,287	12,287	12,287	12,609
Vorarlberg	AT34	16,501	12,470	12,585	12,585	12,585	13,345
Łódzkie	PL11	25,579	53,714	30,944	29,396	21,431	32,213
Mazowieckie	PL12	18,074	32,668	25,289	24,690	16,576	23,459
Małopolskie	PL21	30,551	57,890	35,694	39,469	26,515	38,024
Śląskie	PL22	20,858	44,027	20,768	20,663	15,684	24,400
Lubelskie	PL31	31,533	71,323	45,272	37,693	29,208	43,006
Podkarpackie	PL32	36,859	70,868	35,339	31,288	30,035	40,878
Norte	PT11	21,846	42,676	19,210	19,210	19,113	24,411
Algarve	PT15	11,302	30,386	19,931	11,302	11,302	16,845
Centro (PT)	PT16	19,988	39,046	18,593	18,593	18,542	22,952
Lisboa	PT17	13,987	23,732	19,060	16,477	13,918	17,435
Alentejo	PT18	16,893	35,712	15,765	15,765	12,264	19,280
Slovenija	SI	24,419	30,122	24,284	24,284	24,284	25,479
Bratislavský	SK01	10,585	19,415	19,415	13,459	10,585	14,692
Západné Slovensko	SK02	27,058	47,617	22,964	24,715	22,964	29,064
Stredné Slovensko	SK03	27,715	53,791	28,052	24,133	23,887	31,516
Východné Slovensko	SK04	28,505	59,301	23,584	23,401	21,441	31,246
Itä-Suomi	FI13	20,290	27,930	27,549	26,058	19,646	24,295
Etelä-Suomi	FI18	18,820	18,820	18,820	18,820	18,820	18,820
Länsi-Suomi	FI19	24,615	23,727	24,615	24,615	24,615	24,437
Pohjois-Suomi	FI1A	24,701	21,206	24,701	24,701	24,701	24,002
Stockholm	SE01	10,000	10,000	15,153	15,153	10,000	12,061
Östra Mellansverige	SE02	24,690	20,996	24,690	24,690	24,690	23,951
Sydsverige	SE04	22,775	17,175	22,775	22,775	22,775	21655
Norra Mellansverige	SE06	20,719	15,682	21,455	18,899	20,714	19,494
Mellersta Norrland	SE07	12,185	10,000	21,759	12,391	12,185	13,704
Övre Norrland	SE08	15,154	10,000	22,706	22,706	15,154	17,144
Småland med öarna	SE09	16,494	13,739	20,983	15,501	16,494	16,642
Västsverige	SE0A	21,999	10,000	21,999	21,999	21,999	19,599
South East	UKJ	18,887	11,088	18,887	18,887	18,887	17,327

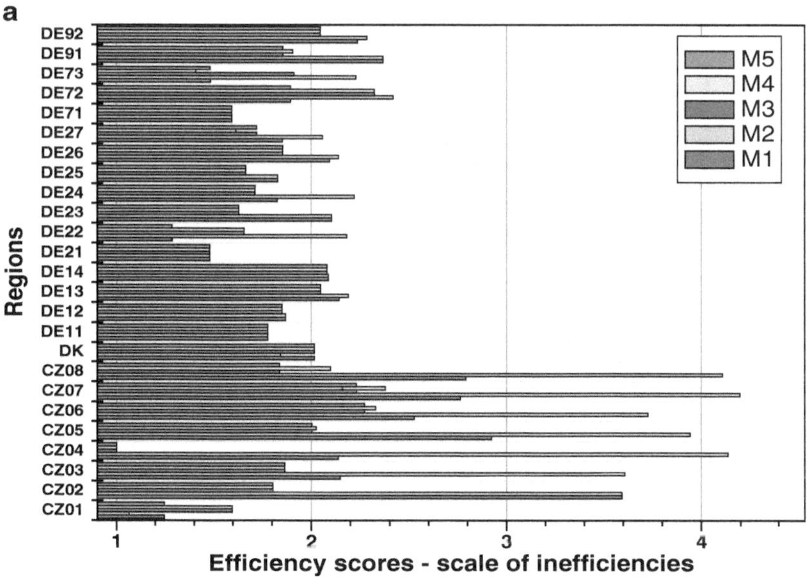

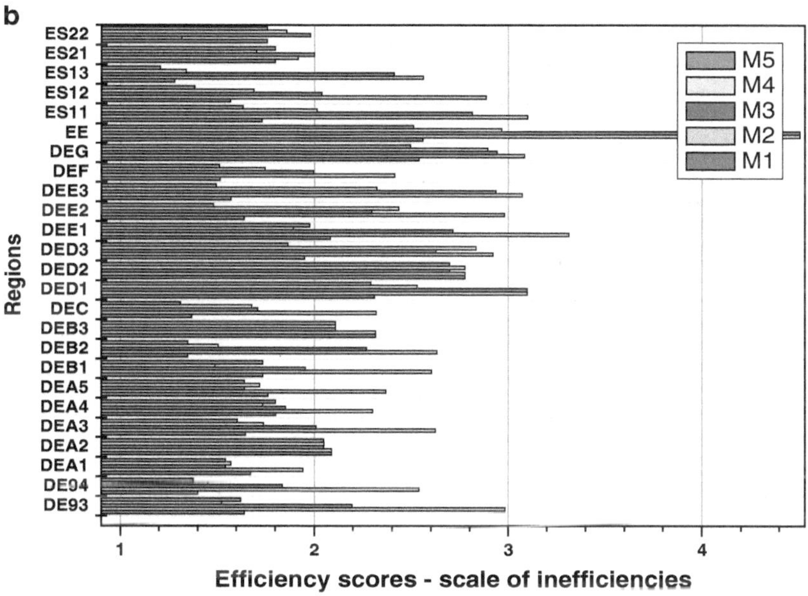

Graph 5.1 (Continued)

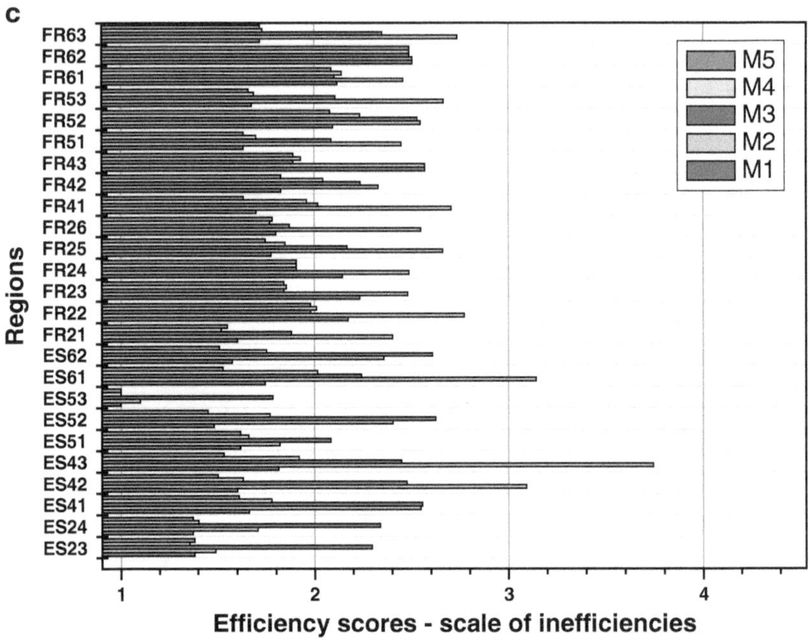

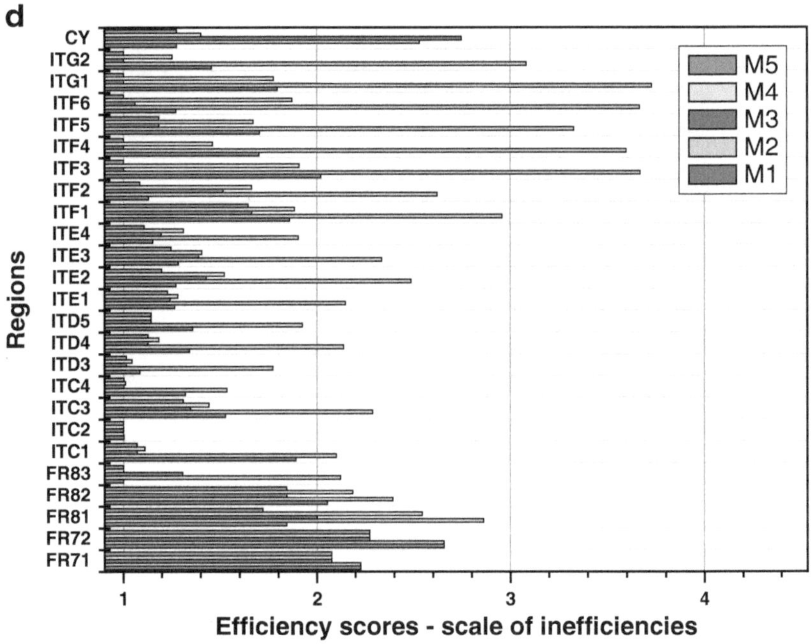

Graph 5.1 (Continued)

e

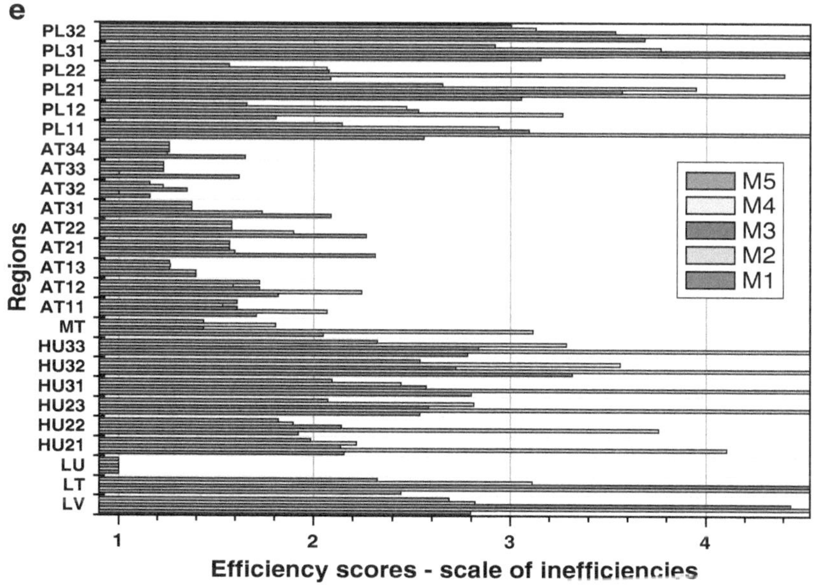

f

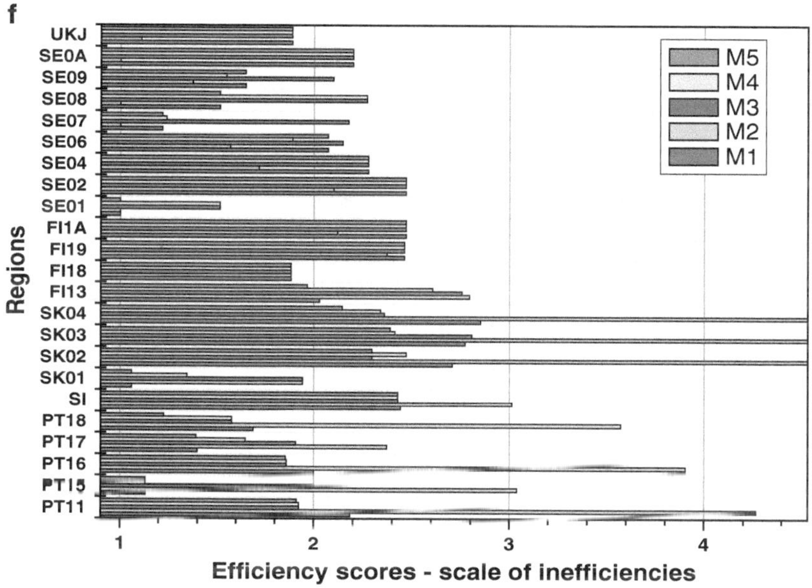

Graph 5.1 Efficiency indicators in M1-M5 chosen regions. (**a**) part 1; (**b**) part 2; (**c**) part 3; (**d**) part 4; (**e**) part 5; (**f**) part 6

Table 5.3 Set of collective fundamental statistical indicators of efficiency in the applied models of DEA

	M1	M2	M3	M4	M5
1. Effective regions (% of population of regions with an efficiency indicator = 1)	2.7%	5.4%	4.7%	3.4%	7.4%
2. Regions with a low inefficiency (% of population of regions with an efficiency indicator of a range of (1;1,5))	19.6%	5.4%	13.5%	18.2%	25.0%
3. Regions with average inefficiency (% of population of regions with an efficiency indicator of a range of (1,5;3))	74.3%	58.8%	76.4%	74.3%	66.9%
4. Regions with a high inefficiency (% of population of regions with an efficiency indicator of >3)	3.4%	30.4%	5.4%	4.1%	0.7%
Maximum inefficiency	3,6859	7,1323	4,7383	3,9469	3,0035
Average efficiency indicator	1,9110	2,7465	2,0421	1,8966	1,7049

In Table 5.3 a set of fundamental collective statistics of all the models has been presented.

In the layout provided above, it was accepted that the efficiency is to be measured with the aid of DEA indicators, which can be distributed in the specified categories depending on the level of these indicators. Taking account of the distribution of the indicators achieved in all the models, it was assumed that the level of inefficiency in the area (1;1,5) is insignificant and is more a result of the variation of scale and economic and demographic nature of the regions. With relation to this, the term of "low inefficiency" was used for their definition. The second group refers to regions with an efficiency in the range of (1,5;3), which clearly falls behind and can be clearly observed in the inappropriate selection of the particular variables. Finally, the last of the groups distinguished refers to regions that are highly inefficient and whose efficiency indicator amounts to above 3. A group of such regions is apart from one exception (the M5 model) more numerous than the groups of regions that are fully efficient. In one of these cases, it is possible to observe a very large number of these groups (the M2 model) and the associated high average degree of inefficiency.

The indicators of efficiency for the M5 model with the indicators for all remaining models have been presented below. The choice of efficiency indicators for the M5 model as a comparative point refers to the fact that in this model the largest number of variables and indicators were taken into consideration in a most complex manner to describe the particular regions of the EU in the area of the features analysed.

Graph 5.2 presents the comparison of efficiency indicators for the M1 and M5 models.

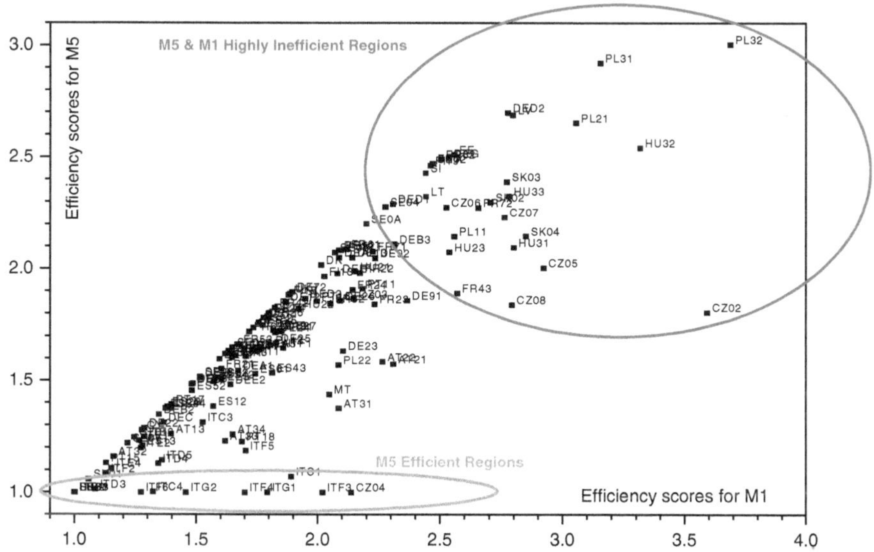

Graph 5.2 Comparison of M1 and M5 efficiency indicators

It is also visible that there are no such regions which could achieve efficiency in the M1 model without achieving efficiency in the M5 model. Apart from that, efficiency is achieved more frequently in the M5 model (11 observations) than in the case of the M1 model (only four observations). The scale of this inefficiency is comparable in both models, although insignificantly higher results or in other words, higher inefficiency can be observed in the case of the M1 model, which confirms both the observations of maximum and average values.

In Graph 5.3, the indicators of the M2 model with the indicators of the M5 have been displayed. In this case, the correlation is not so obvious. In both cases there is relatively the most efficient units, but however they differ in terms of the scale of inefficiency which is decidedly not in favour of the M2 model. Regions achieving efficiency in one of the models are frequently highly inefficient in another (examples of this are the CZ04 or SE0A regions). an explanation of this variation can also be the fact that the construction of the M2 model used particular inputs such as the level of unemployment and long term unemployment. Both of these variables were not included in the M5 model, which was connected with industry and the

> The first observation is that of the significant correlation of results in both models. This correlation can certify that the variable inputs used in the M1 model, or in other words, employment in industry, as well as expenditure on R&D, are of large significance for the creation of GDP in the regions. what is symptomatic is the fact that none of the regions achieves a greater efficiency in the M1 model than in the M5 model. This is confirmed by the theory presented above referring to the essence of the variables used in the M1 model.

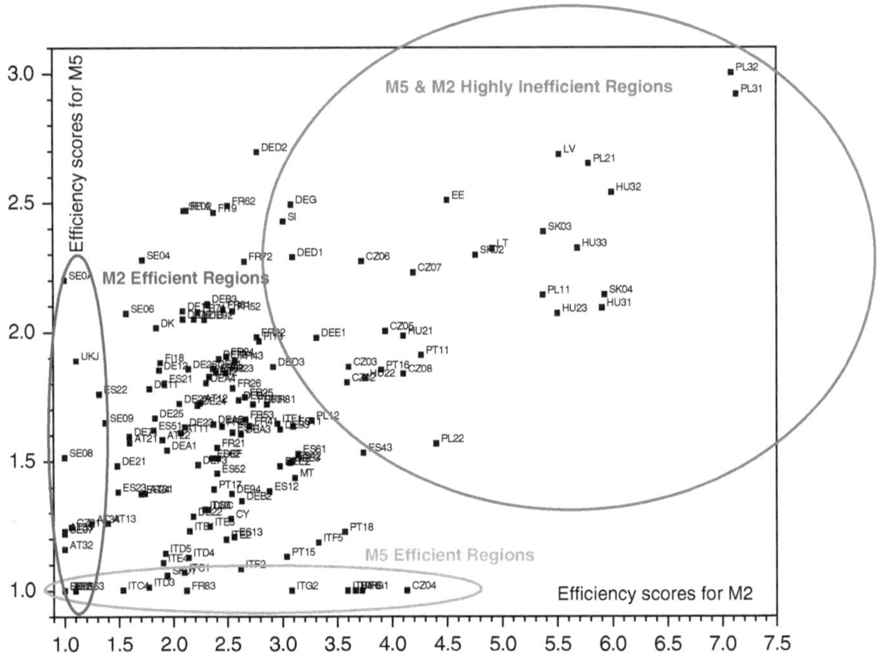

Graph 5.3 Comparison of M2 and M5 efficiency indicators

phenomenon of unemployment itself does not directly carry over to the category of specific sectors.

Graph 5.4 presents a comparison of the efficiency indicators for the M3 and M5 models.

As in the case of the first set presented, a significant correlation of efficiency indicators is evident in both models. This time however, the efficiency indicators in the M3 model are even lower. As in the previous case, this correlation can certify that the variable inputs used in the M3 model, or in other words, employment in the production sector, as well as a higher level of education are of large significance in the creation of GDP in regions.

As in the case of the M1 model, the level of variables used in the M3 model is less favourable for regions than for instance the M2 and M3 models and this can have a significant impact on the worsening of their efficiency. It is also visible that there are no regions which could achieve efficiency in the M3 model without achieving efficiency in the M5 model.

The next comparison refers to the M4 and M5 models. As evident in Graph 5.5, once again we are faced with two phenomena: *the correlation of efficiency indicators in both models, as well as the lower scale of inefficiency in a more complex model (M5) in comparison to a simpler model (M4).*

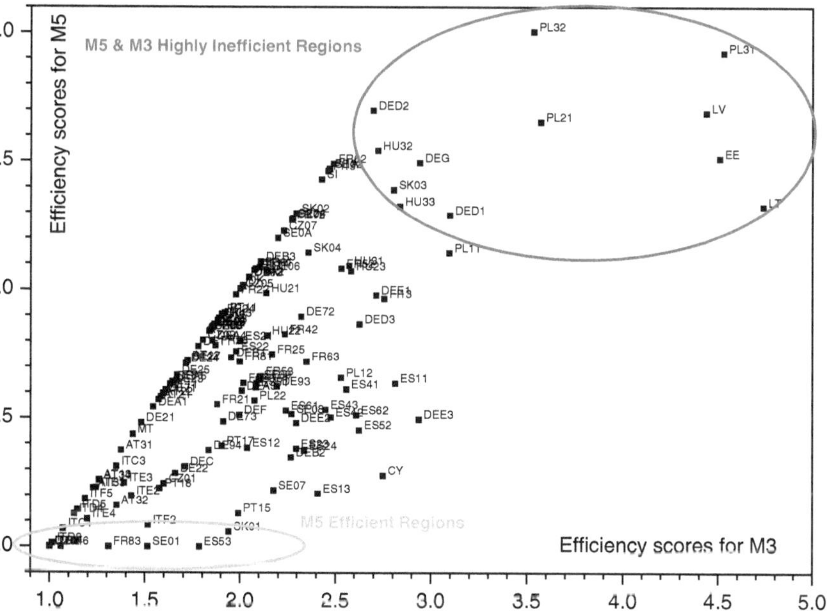

Graph 5.4 Comparison of M3 and M5 efficiency indicators

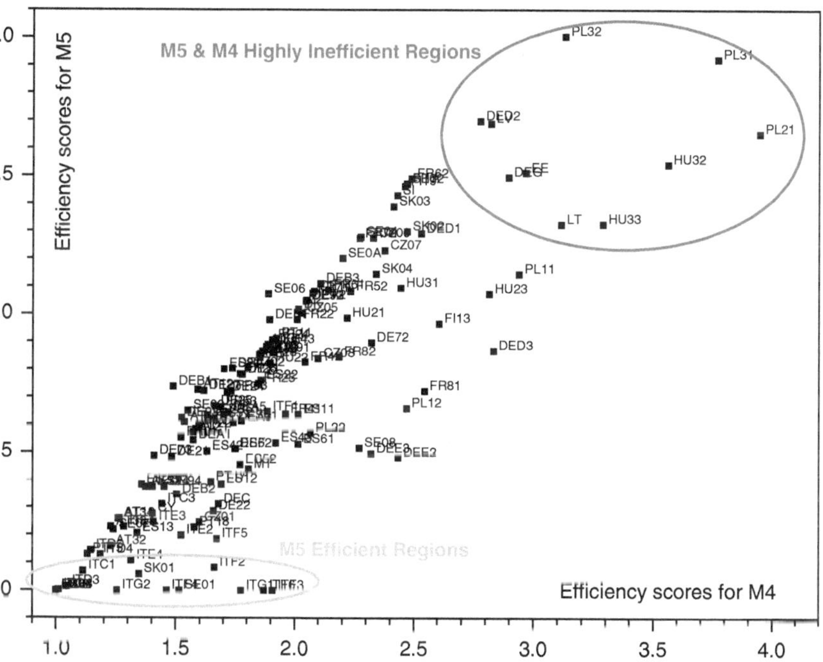

Graph 5.5 Comparison of M4 and M5 efficiency indicators

The novelty of this comparison is the existence of such regions which have a higher efficiency in the M4 model than in the M5 model (such a phenomenon was visible in the case of the M2 model, but then the M5 model did not avail of all its variables). This means that the level of expenditure on R&D can have a positive impact on the creation of GDP in regions.

5.2 Identification of EU Regional Efficiency Clusters

5.2.1 K-Means Model Methodology in Regional Clustering

The aim of the second stage of the research is the introduction of new characteristics to the set of variables serving to mark out the efficiency of the regions and carry out their recategorization. The introduction of new variables serves to first of all achieve the main aim of this paper which is to identify the network phenomena occurring in the regions and define their approximate impact or relation to efficiency.

For the realization of the aims of the second stage the k-means method was used. Categorization with the aid of this method is carried out by the acceptance of assumptions referring to the numbers of the groups and subsequently the initiation of the optimizing algorithm which leads to the standardization of the composition of particular groups. Finally, such procedures that are carried out leads to the acquisition of standardized groups with regard to the variables used. The application of the k-means for the categorization of regions is not novel as a similar methodology was used by among others, Blien,[17] Perugii i Signorelli,[18] Marelli[19] and Aumayr.[20] It is therefore possible to acknowledge that this methodology is tried and trusted and widely acknowledged as appropriate for realizing this type of categorization.

The innovativeness of applying this methodology in the case of research carried out in this dissertation involves the use of the network variable for this categorization.

The construction of the algorithm in the k-means method itself is not complicated. The fundamental assumption is that for a specified population (in this case

[17]Blien et al. (2006).

[18]Perugini and Signorelli (2004).

[19]Marelli (2007).

[20]Aumayr (2007).

EU regions at the level of NUTS 2) marks out the number of groups in which particular units can be divided. Initially, each unit is divided into non-specific groups. Grouping with the k-means clustering method is carried out with the repeated application of a two-stage process in which:

> The average vector is calculated for each unit in each grouping.
> These units are repeatedly divided up into groups whose centres are the nearest units.

This process is repeated until the particular units stop changing groups in the second stage. After the conclusion of the process, the number of groups with a standardized nature of the units belonging to them is achieved.

With the categorization of the k-means the average square distance of the unit x_k from the centre of its nearest grouping is calculated as follows:

$$E_K = \sum_k \left\| x_k - m_{c(x_k)} \right\|^2 \tag{5.26}$$

where $c(x_k)$ is the index of the centre of the grouping nearest to x_k. The algorithm starts from the set of K centres of groups marked as m_i, $i = 1,\ldots,K$. Following this, the location of m_i is in an iterative manner applied to the assigned units and subsequently the centres are recounted. The iteration is completed if E does not change significantly.[21]

> Key significance in the process of the categorization of regions is therefore held by marking out the variables for the realization. In this paper it has been assumed that for the requirements of categorizing regions two variables were used: *the parameter of efficiency and the parameter of networking*. With relation to this, as the result of Stage I (Sect. 5.1) the analysis carried out is a range of indicators of efficiency for each region covered by the analysis, in which it was decided to calculate the values of the average indicator of efficiency for all five models.

The average efficiency indicator illustrates the general scope of inefficiency of the region (only Luxembourg is efficient in all five models), taking account of all the categories in the construction of the models. The average indicator does not refer to the absolute efficiency of the region in the formation of the level of GDP but only indicates its efficiency in using the variables with regard to other regions analysed in the research. Therefore, it is possible to state that the average efficiency indicator constitutes its own ranking in terms of regions analysed with regard to various aspects of efficiency.

[21] http://www.cis.hut.fi/~sami/thesis/node9.html

The average efficiency indicator constitutes the basis for using the second variable for the categorization of the k-means method with regard to the network variable. The identification of such variables itself constitutes a difficult task. Taking account of the fact that the accessibility of statistical data for regions at the level of NUTS 2 is limited, there was no significant choice in this regard. The "Focus" indicator was therefore used for this purpose.

In deciding on the quantitative methodology used based on statistical data, it is necessary to be aware that up to now a set of constant indicators has not been established which would be the most reliable and valuable in the assessment of cluster structures. The definition and subsequent marking out of values for the set of indicators which serve to monitor the development of clusters is important for two reasons. Clear results facilitate the evaluation of the impact of clusters on economic development and competitiveness of a given location. On the other hand, indicator analysis facilitates the realization of the assessment of benchmarking in a regional dimension, which in effect leads to the strengthening of the abilities to monitor the realization of innovative policies based on clusters e.g. at the level of EU regions.

The definition of the determinants of development of clusters in various regions with regard to one economic group is activity which leads to the identification of stronger and weaker regions with relation to sectoral competitiveness. As a result, it is possible to define the desired directions of public intervention within the framework of coherent policies of reducing inter-regional disproportion.

The indicator of concentration for clusters can be defined as the measurement of the concentration or domination of sectoral clusters in the region. Its value is based on the indicators of employment and is calculated in the result for the application of the following equation:

$$D_{r,s} = e_{r,s}/E_r$$

where $D_{r,s}$ – the degree of domination of the sectoral cluster s in the regional economy r; $e_{r,s}$ – the number of employed in the sectoral cluster s in the region r; E_r –the total number of employed in all sectors of the economy in the region r

It is necessary to remember that the high value of the indicator is not equal to the biggest participation of a given sectoral cluster in the creation of economic value in the economy. In this area, it is necessary to be aware of certain restrictions in using quantitative indicators based on the number of people employed in sectoral clusters in evaluating their economic potential. Particularly sectoral clusters are characterized by various economic productivity and labour efficiency. However, on the other hand, the indicators based on employment are becoming the most convenient in the identification and assessment of clusters due to the relatively easy access to statistical data in this area at particular levels of EU administrative units. In effect, the application of this type of indicators accounting for the final synthetic measurements favour the clusters with a high level of employment. The indicator of the employment concentration used is therefore to a certain extent burdened by the existing differences in the intensity of using the labour force between various categories of clusters. That is also why it would be advisable to use the supplementary data also referring to productivity or value added in the evaluation of clusters. The results achieved in this way would be very favourable for the clusters from the sectors with a high degree of using knowledge, such as IT, communications and biopharmaceutical branches.

The barrier mentioned above is successfully reduced by including first of all the DEA coefficients into the analysis, which take account of the fractional indicators in their structure referring to socio-economic aspects in the dimension of inputs and effects. The $D_{r,s}$ indicator is immediately used as a variable illustrating the intensity of transforming the economy of the region into an economy based on network interaction. This is a reference point and an essential element in the complex socio-economic analysis in the context of an emerging network economy in EU regions. The desired results of the research are generated thanks to the interaction and mutual reference to values of the two categories of indicators.

Due to the restriction in the access to the desired statistical data the employment indicator used was fully justified and does not constitute a barrier in the interpretation of the expected results. The value of the indicator should be viewed first of all as a variable that enables the assessment of the range and degree of occurrence of network interaction in the dimension of spatial arrangements. The subject of the analysis is not the economic results of the regions analysed as this type of variable is included in the set of indicators used for the calculation of the DEA coefficients of efficiency. The results gained for all the indicators used in the analysis provide as a result the basis for analysing the aspects of socio-economic cohesion in EU regions in the context of the network economy.

The acceptance of the aforementioned indicator should be acknowledged as appropriate in this book, which is confirmed by both the practice of its application in similar research projects, but also the utilitarianism gained for its value which in effect, gives the opportunity of the desired interpretation. If a given cluster indicates a significant share in the total employment in a regional economy, there is a big probability of spontaneous emergence of network interactions and external effects (spillover effects) within the framework of a given sector instead of absorption or in other words "melting" in interactions occurring in different segments of the regional economy. The value of the indicator illustrates the degree by which the economy of the region is oriented on the sector, which is represented by a given cluster. It is usually assumed that in the case where the level of employment in a given cluster does not exceed 1,000 people it is not taken into consideration in the analysis in order to avoid the risk of including a cluster which is too insignificant in the economy of the region. The optimal value of the indicator for the cluster is deemed to be the level of from 7% of the share of employment in the enterprises of the cluster in terms of the total employment in the economy of a given location.[22]

[22]The value was accepted in the assessment of sectoral clusters in the report on research carried out on the level of new EU member countries: Ketels and Sölvell (2006).

This is a result which can facilitate the definition of a given cluster in terms of the dominant one in question. The region in which the territory is identified as a cluster with the highest value of the $D_{r,s}$ indicator can be seen as dominated by a given sector of the economy, as the greatest amount of professionally active people working in it. This sector of the economy shall be characterized by potentially the largest number of network interactions between enterprises. However, this assumption should not be considered as a rigid rule as a large number of employed people in a given sector does not mean that it is filled with a large number of associated enterprises. The sector illustrating a large share of employment in the regional economy can be dominated by a few large enterprises involved in the total amount of labour force in the region. It is always necessary to take account of this aspect in the interpretation of results which has been done here in this book.

In accordance with the quality assumption, the identification of sectoral clusters in the regions analysed and the calculation of their values for the indicators of dominance in terms of employment has been carried out. This type of indicator was marked out for EU regions at the level of NUTS II as a result of research carried out within the framework of the *Cluster Observatory* project. In the dimension of each region, groups of various sectoral clusters were identified and a subjective indicator was worked out for them. From the point of view of the assumptions of the accepted methodology, the desired research is the totalling of all the indicators for the individual clusters in terms of each region. In this way, the accumulated share of employment in sectoral clusters of the region is marked out in terms of general employment figures in the regional economy. As a result, such an analysis illustrates the degree of saturation of cluster structures in the economy of the region.

It is possible to accept that the greater value of the total indicators $D_{r,s}$ for all the identified clusters shall then mean a greater range in the occurrence of network interaction in the economy of the region. These same regions which are characterized by a large dynamism of growth, given as $D_{r,s}$ in terms of the value of the indicators are directed towards achieving a state in the economy which is more based on sectoral networks of interaction. In some European regions, these values can even reach scores of percentage points, which means that the regional economy is dominated by highly specialized sectoral clusters.

5.2.2 Presentation and Interpretation of Research Results

In Table 5.4, the values of both variables for the particular regions have been presented, while being ordered in a rising fashion with regard to the average efficiency indicator.

Having such prepared variables the next dilemma was the marking out of a number of groups. With relation to this, the fundamental aim of the research in

Table 5.4 Average efficiency indicator and the focus on the regions

Nazwa	Symbol	Index DEA	Focus
Luxembourg (Grand-Duché)	LU	10,000	0.1873
Valle d'Aosta/Vallée d'Aoste	ITC2	10,004	0.1943
Lombardia	ITC4	11,744	0.4590
Illes Balears	ES53	11,767	0.2180
Salzburg	AT32	11,795	0.1474
Veneto	ITD3	11,860	0.4013
Stockholm	SE01	12,061	0.2400
Tirol	AT33	12,609	0.2616
Corse	FR83	12,859	0.1901
Wien	AT13	13,156	0.2169
Vorarlberg	AT34	13,345	0.1890
Lazio	ITE4	13,345	0.2394
Emilia-Romagna	ITD5	13,432	0.3389
Praha	CZ01	13,499	0.2263
Mellersta Norrland	SE07	13,704	0.1264
Friuli-Venezia Giulia	ITD4	13,844	0.2358
Toscana	ITE1	14,339	0.2643
Piemonte	ITC1	14,486	0.3316
Bratislavský	SK01	14,692	0.1871
Oberbayern	DE21	14,826	0.3498
Marche	ITE3	15,333	0.2215
Sardegna	ITG2	15,591	0.1187
La Rioja	ES23	15,808	0.2056
Umbria	ITE2	15,819	0.1641
Liguria	ITC3	15,843	0.1498
Oberösterreich	AT31	15,900	0.2484
Darmstadt	DE71	15,958	0.1568
Molise	ITF2	16,033	0.1315
Niederbayern	DE22	16,144	0.2893
Aragón	ES24	16,391	0.1455
Düsseldorf	DEA1	16,551	0.3227
Småland med öarna	SE09	16,642	0.2021
Saarland	DEC	16,773	0.3768
Algarve	PT15	16,845	0.2766
Kassel	DE73	17,050	0.2533
Burgenland	AT11	17,061	0.1285
Övre Norrland	SE08	17,144	0.0701
Weser-Ems	DE94	17,198	0.2922
Kärnten	AT21	17,249	0.2035
Mittelfranken	DE25	17,319	0.3443
South East	UKJ	17,327	0.1735
Comunidad Foral de Navarra	ES22	17,349	0.1701
Lisboa	PT17	17,435	0.2729
Puglia	ITF4	17,521	0.0963
Cantabria	ES13	17,587	0.1404
Cataluña	ES51	17,608	0.3989
Calabria	ITF6	17,738	0.0465
Stuttgart	DE11	17,798	0.4557
Steiermark	AT22	17,824	0.2343
Champagne-Ardenne	FR21	17,922	0.1870
Schwaben	DE27	17,944	0.3381

(continued)

Table 5.4 (continued)

Nazwa	Symbol	Index DEA	Focus
Basilicata	ITF5	18,151	0.1181
Trier	DEB2	18,198	0.2079
Niederösterreich	AT12	18,208	0.0724
Oberpfalz	DE23	18,211	0.3878
Arnsberg	DEA5	18,274	0.3434
Schleswig-Holstein	DEF	18,368	0.1454
Oberfranken	DE24	18,386	0.3445
País Vasco	ES21	18,446	0.1759
Kýpros/Kbrs	CY	18,471	0.2497
Severozápad	CZ04	18,549	0.2497
Karlsruhe	DE12	18,590	0.3349
Sicilia	ITG1	18,597	0.0936
Etelä-Suomi	FI18	18,820	0.2352
Detmold	DEA4	18,994	0.3508
Pays de la Loire	FR51	19,009	0.1885
Koblenz	DEB1	19,038	0.2093
Principado de Asturias	ES12	19,140	0.1432
Campania	ITF3	19,200	0.1255
Münster	DEA3	19,255	0.0000
Alentejo	PT18	19,280	0.2348
Comunidad Valenciana	ES52	19,472	0.2678
Norra Mellansverige	SE06	19,494	0.1470
Bourgogne	FR26	19,550	0.1533
Västsverige	SE0A	19,599	0.1329
Poitou-Charentes	FR53	19,602	0.1697
Unterfranken	DE26	19,604	0.3297
Región de Murcia	ES62	19,613	0.1437
Malta	MT	19,693	0.2780
Danmark	DK	19,817	0.3118
Lüneburg	DE93	19,931	0.1979
Abruzzo	ITF1	20,023	0.0467
Lorraine	FR41	20,038	0.1905
Castilla y León	ES41	20,309	0.1827
Basse-Normandie	FR25	20,406	0.1398
Haute-Normandie	FR23	20,503	0.2510
Limousin	FR63	20,514	0.1630
Alsace	FR42	20,522	0.1666
Castilla-La Mancha	ES42	20,612	0.1202
Provence-Alpes-Côte d'Azur	FR82	20,640	0.1357
Köln	DEA2	20,657	0.2829
Centre	FR24	20,698	0.1799
Braunschweig	DE91	20,714	0.3431
Tübingen	DE14	20,843	0.2767
Freiburg	DE13	20,957	0.2824
Hannover	DE92	21,327	0.2238
Andalucía	ES61	21,351	0.2210
Rhône-Alpes	FR71	21,352	0.2932
Sydsverige	SE04	21,655	0.0666
Halle	DEE2	21,662	0.2412
Franche-Comté	FR43	21,701	0.2858
Gießen	DE72	21,706	0.2708

(*continued*)

Table 5.4 (continued)

Nazwa	Symbol	Index DEA	Focus
Aquitaine	FR61	21,813	0.1594
Picardie	FR22	21,830	0.1957
Rheinhessen-Pfalz	DEB3	21,914	0.2909
Languedoc-Roussillon	FR81	21,942	0.1041
Galicia	ES11	22,589	0.1834
Jihozápad	CZ03	22,703	0.2563
Magdeburg	DEE3	22,791	0.1551
Extremadura	ES43	22,921	0.1037
Centro (PT)	PT16	22,952	0.3152
Bretagne	FR52	22,976	0.1989
Nyugat-Dunántúl	HU22	23,082	0.2108
Mazowieckie	PL12	23,459	0.3062
Östra Mellansverige	SE02	23,951	0.1354
Dessau	DEE1	23,961	0.2361
Pohjois-Suomi	FI1A	24,002	0.1656
Auvergne	FR72	24,262	0.1622
Itä-Suomi	FI13	24,295	0.0784
Leipzig	DED3	24,392	0.1964
Śląskie	PL22	24,400	0.2995
Norte	PT11	24,411	0.3887
Länsi-Suomi	FI19	24,437	0.1276
Midi-Pyrénées	FR62	24,954	0.1816
Střední Čechy	CZ02	25,198	0.2115
Közép-Dunántúl	HU21	25,205	0.2548
Moravskoslezsko	CZ08	25,351	0.2170
Slovenija	SI	25,479	0.2462
Severovýchod	CZ05	25,800	0.2876
Jihovýchod	CZ06	26,257	0.1968
Chemnitz	DED1	26,645	0.2782
Dresden	DED2	27,443	0.2021
Střední Morava	CZ07	27,597	0.2260
Thüringen	DEG	27,900	0.2350
Západné Slovensko	SK02	29,064	0.2317
Dél-Dunántúl	HU23	31,020	0.1339
Východné Slovensko	SK04	31,246	0.1664
Stredné Slovensko	SK03	31,516	0.1647
Észak-Magyarország	HU31	31,635	0.1535
Łódzkie	PL11	32,213	0.3399
Dél-Alföld	HU33	33,829	0.1246
Eesti	EE	34,096	0.2444
Lietuva	LT	35,063	0.3318
Észak-Alföld	HU32	36,270	0.1098
Latvija	LV	36,530	0.2108
Małopolskie	PL21	38,024	0.2645
Podkarpackie	PL32	40,878	0.2759
Lubelskie	PL31	43,006	0.3040

marking out the impact of networking on the efficiency of regions does not need to create many groups to verify this theory. It is possible to assume that each of the parameters can take on a high value or a low value. In carrying out the categorization of the regions with the assumptions achieved for the four groupings of regions presented above, the numbers for the particular groups were 40, 24, 55 and 29 respectively for the regions. The basic factor differentiating the regions is the average value of both variables used for their categorization. It is necessary to emphasize that the closer to 1 the value of the first of the variables used is (the so-called average efficiency indicator), the greater the efficiency. The second variable, which is the Focus indicator, is not a varying value and only indicates the involvement at the level of regions in the functioning of clusters. In Table 5.5, the results of the categorization carried out have been presented, as well as the calculation of the average of both variables for the particular groups.

In order to get a better illustration of the differences in the value of the variables between the particular units, all of them have been presented together with the indicated categorization in Graph 5.6.

In the four separate graphs (Graph 5.7a–d), the position of EU regions is presented which shows the variation of socio-economic coherence in the dimension of efficiency and networking.

It is clearly visible that *return correlation exists* between the variables. The greater the average efficiency indicator, the lower the Focus indicator is. It is possible therefore to come to the conclusion from the categorization carried out that *large involvement in the functioning of network structures in a given region is associated with high efficiency of the region in question, which was the issue of the research and the theory presented in this dissertation* (Graph 5.8).

5.3 Summary of Research Results

5.3.1 *Verification of Findings Using the Self Organizing Map* Method

For the verification of the results gained, the grouping of the regions was repeated by using the same criteria but introducing a modification of the methodology applied. The *Self Organizing Maps (SOM)* method was applied for this purpose.

The function which was used for realizing the algorithm of categorization with the SOM method has the following form:

$$E = \sum_k \sum_i h_{ci} \|x_k - m_i\|^2 \tag{5.27}$$

Table 5.5 Categorization of regions with the "k-means" method in four groupings

Group 1			Group 2			Group 3			Group 4		
Regions	Effectivness indicator	Focus network indicator	Regions	Effectivness factor	Focus network indicator	Regions	Effectivness indicator	Focus network indicator	Regions	Effectivness indicator	Focus network indicator
CZ01	13,499	0.2263	DE11	17,798	0.4557	SI	25.479	0.2462	SE0A	19,599	0.1329
FR83	12,859	0.1901	ES53	11,767	0.2180	SK02	29,064	0.2317	FR72	24,262	0.1622
AT34	13.345	0.1890	LU	10.000	0.1873	PL31	43,006	0.3040	SE08	17,144	0.0701
PL12	23.459	0.3062	ITD5	13,432	0.3389	ITF2	16,033	0.1315	SE04	21,655	0.0666
PL22	24,400	0.2995	SE01	12,061	0.2400	SE07	13,704	0.1264	SK04	31,246	0.1664
PT16	22,952	0.3152	ITE4	13,345	0.2394	ITE2	15,819	0.1641	FI13	24,295	0.0784
PT15	16,845	0.2766	ITE1	14,339	0.2643	LT	35,063	0.3318	SE02	23,951	0.1354
AT31	15,900	0.2484	ITD3	11,860	0.4013	HU22	23,082	0.2108	FI19	24,437	0.1276
DEB3	21,914	0.2909	ITC4	11,744	0.4590	HU21	25,205	0.2548	FI1A	24,002	0.1656
DEB2	18,198	0.2079	ITC2	10,004	0.1943	PL11	32,213	0.3399	ES43	22,921	0.1037
PT17	17,435	0.2729	DEA1	16,551	0.3227	SE06	19,494	0.1470	FR25	20,406	0.1398
AT32	11,795	0.1474	ITC1	14,486	0.3316	ITG2	15,591	0.1187	DEA3	19,255	0.0000
AT21	17,249	0.2035	DE12	18,590	0.3349	PL21	38,024	0.2645	ES42	20,612	0.1202
AT22	17,824	0.2343	DEA5	18,274	0.3434	AT11	17,051	0.1285	AT12	18,208	0.0724
DEA2	20,657	0.2829	DE21	14,826	0.3498	FR62	24,954	0.1816	HU32	36,270	0.1098
ITE3	15,333	0.2215	DEC	16,773	0.3768	UKJ	17,327	0.1735	HU33	33,829	0.1246
FR71	21,352	0.2932	DE25	17,319	0.3443	EE	34,096	0.2444	LV	36,530	0.2108
ITD4	13,844	0.2358	DE24	18,386	0.3445	DEE2	21,662	0.2412	HU31	31,635	0.1535
FR43	21,701	0.2858	DEA4	18,994	0.3508	DEF	18,368	0.1454	FR81	21,942	0.1041
CY	18,471	0.2497	DE27	17,944	0.3381	DEG	27,900	0.2350	ITF6	17,738	0.0465
FR23	20,503	0.2510	DE22	16,144	0.2893	ES11	22,589	0.1834	ITG1	18,597	0.0936
ES23	15,808	0.2056	DE23	18,211	0.3878	DED3	24,392	0.1964	ITF1	20,023	0.0467
ES52	19,472	0.2678	AT33	12,609	0.2616	ES12	19,140	0.1432	PL32	40,878	0.2759
MT	19,693	0.2780	ITC3	15,843	0.1498	ES13	17,587	0.1404	HU23	31,020	0.1339
AT13	13,156	0.2169	**Average**	**15,054**	**0.3135**	ES21	18,446	0.1759	ITF4	17,521	0.0963
PT18	19,280	0.2348	**Regions**		**24**	DEE1	23,961	0.2361	ITF3	19,200	0.1255
PT11	24,411	0.3887				DED1	26,645	0.2782	ITF5	18,151	0.1181
DE13	20,957	0.2824				DED2	27,443	0.2021	DEE3	22,791	0.1551

(*continued*)

Table 5.5 (continued)

Group 1			Group 2			Group 3			Group 4		
Regions	Effectivness indicator	Focus network indicator	Regions	Effectivness factor	Focus network indicator	Regions	Effectivness indicator	Focus network indicator	Regions	Effectivness indicator	Focus network indicator
DE72	21,706	0.2708				ES41	20,309	0.1827	FR82	20,640	0.1357
DE26	19,604	0.3297				CZ07	27,597	0.2260	**Average**	**24,095**	**0.1197**
DK	19,817	0.3118				CZ03	22,703	0.2563	**Regions**		**29**
DE94	17,198	0.2922				CZ05	25,800	0.2876			
CZ04	18,549	0.2497				CZ06	26,257	0.1968			
DE73	17,050	0.2533				CZ08	25,351	0.2170			
FI18	18,820	0.2352				DEB1	19,038	0.2093			
DE14	20,843	0.2767				DE71	15,958	0.1568			
SK01	14,692	0.1871				DE92	21,327	0.2238			
DE91	20,714	0.3431				DE93	19,931	0.1979			
SE09	16,642	0.2021				ES24	16,391	0.1455			
ES51	17,608	0.3989				ES22	17,349	0.1701			
Average	**18,389**	**0.2613**				FR41	20,038	0.1905			
Regions		**40**				FR53	19,602	0.1697			
						FR24	20,698	0.1799			
						FR61	21,813	0.1594			
						FR52	22,976	0.1989			
						FR21	17,922	0.1870			
						FR51	19,009	0.1885			
						FR26	19,550	0.1533			
						FR42	20,522	0.1666			
						FR22	21,830	0.1957			
						FR63	20,514	0.1630			
						ES61	21,351	0.2210			
						CZ02	25,198	0.2115			
						ES62	19,613	0.1437			
						SK03	31,516	0.1647			
						Average	**22,791**	**0.1989**			
						Regions		**55**			

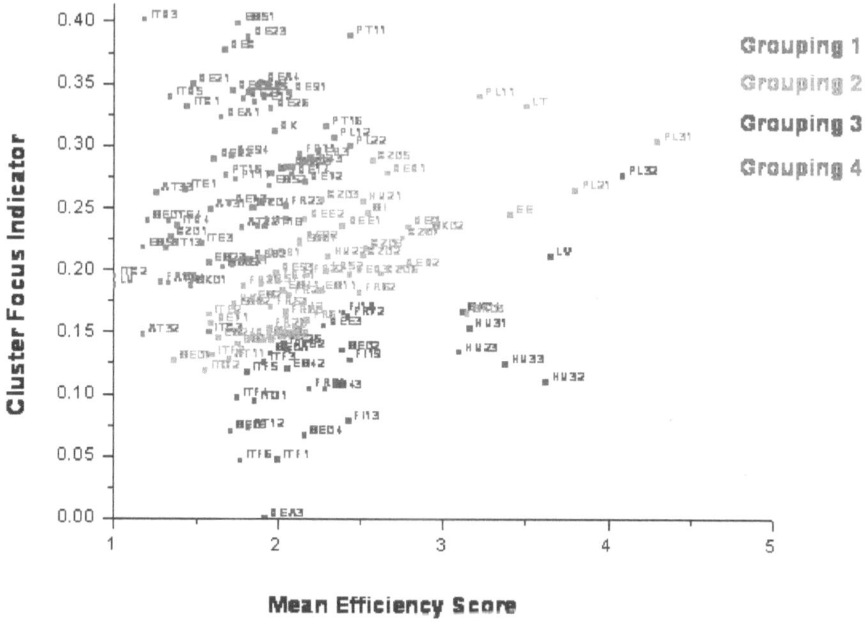

Graph 5.6 Position of EU regions established by the *K-means* method with the assumption of four groupings

Where the c index is dependent on the values of x_k and the reference vectors m_i. The iteration procedure is carried out by the gradual minimization of the function:

$$E_1 = \sum_i h_{ci} \|x(t) - m_i\|^2 \tag{5.28}$$

The random choice of samples *x(t)* gave an iteration of *t*. This function subsequently corresponds to the next step of conjectural approximation of the minimum as in (5.27).[23] The function (5.27) SOM is very similar to the function (5.26), whose algorithm of k-means minimizes. The difference is that the SOM takes account of the distance of each unit from each reference vector (grouping centre) and not only from the nearest one as in the case of the k-means method.[24]

A detailed illustration of the units entering the composition of groups gained by the SOM method is presented in Table 5.6. The assigned method of SOM as regards grouping is automatically laid out in decreasing form according to the values of the average efficiency indicator. Taking account of the composition of the groups or the average of both variables gained, it is possible to compare the grouping gained by

[23] http://www.cis.hut.fi/~sami/thesis/node25.html

[24] http://www.cis.hut.fi/~sami/thesis/node26.html

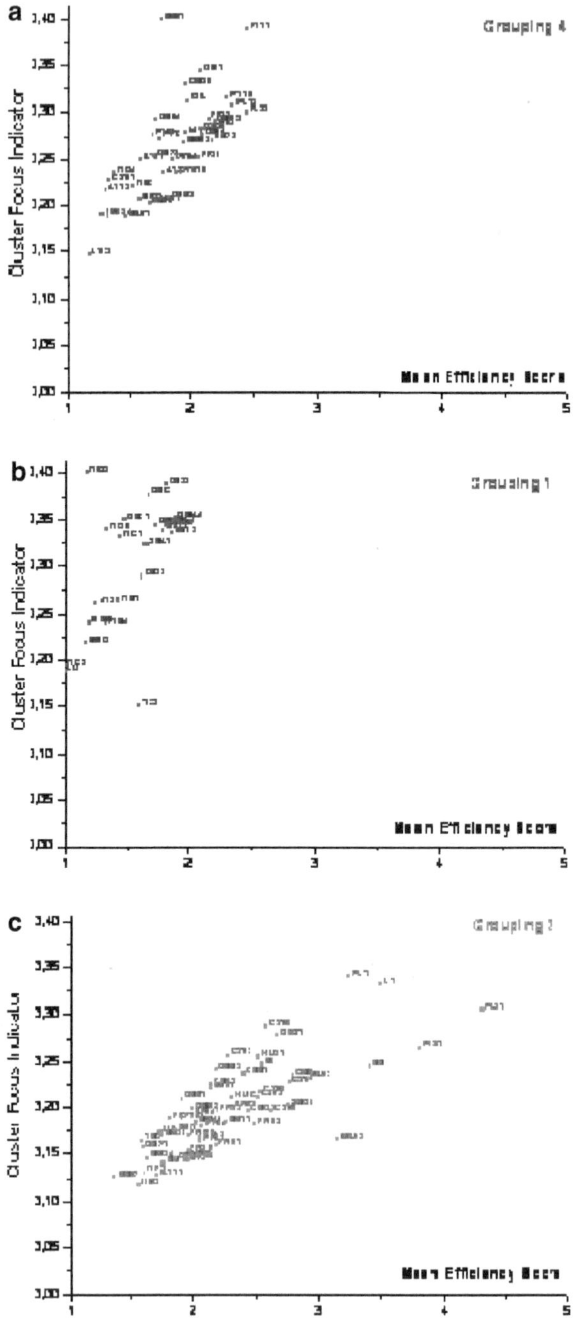

Graph 5.7 (Continued)

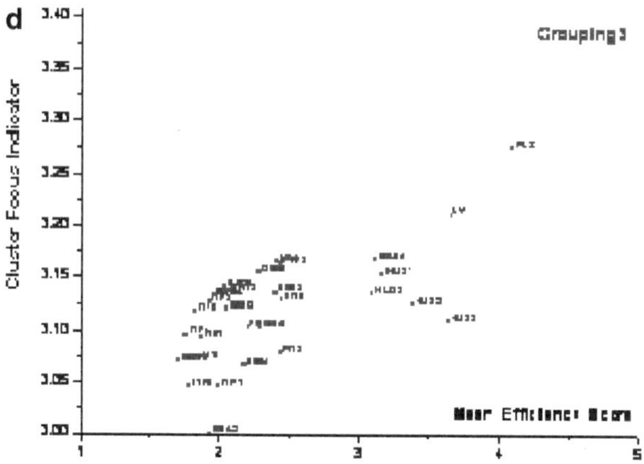

Graph 5.7 Position of EU regions belonging groups established by the *K-means* method. (**a**) group 1; (**b**) group 2; (**c**) group 3; (**d**) group 4

this method with those gained by the k-means method. It is possible to mark out the equivalents in both sets by using these parameters. In this way, group 0 from SOM matches group 4 gained in the categorization method of k-means, group 1 (SOM) group 3, group 2 (SOM) group 1 and group 3 (SOM) group 2. These groups are of a similar nature in general, but however differ in the amount of associated regions and their composition.

In Graph 5.9, the categorization of EU regions is illustrated and realized with the aid of the supporting method of SOM. As can be seen, the location of the group is very similar to that of the k-means method and the differences that occur in the composition of the group and the degree of their adjustment. The penetration of groups does not occur here as in the previous case, which is confirmed by the theory of better adjustment of elements in the particular groups.

In Table 5.7, the basic statistics are gained in the categorization with the aid of both methods. The statistics used are average, standard deviations, standard errors, minimum, maximum and the range of two variables in the particular groups.

The differences between the results achieved by the application of research methods are insignificant and not directed, which means that in particular cases a greater deviation or errors occurs once in the case of one method and once in the case of the other. It should be therefore assumed that the results achieved can be acknowledged as significant for each of the categorizations carried out.

It is also possible to relate this to regions that change their classification by changes in the methods of categorization. It should be acknowledged that regions which are found in the lower group of classification have the potential to improve this classification. Of course, the interests of the given region does not lie in the fact of changing its classification but in improving the efficiency in working out GDP,

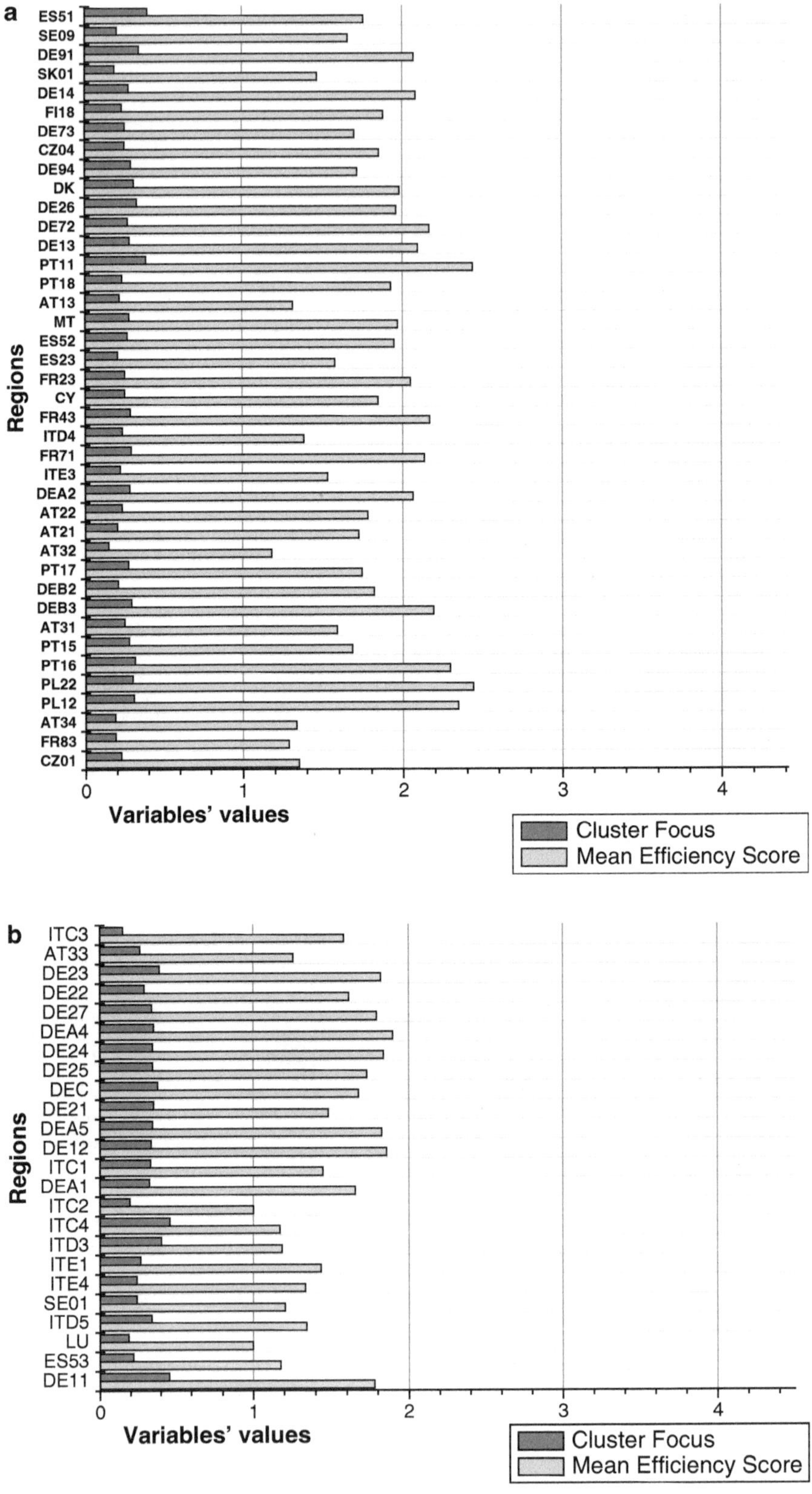

Graph 5.8 (Continued)

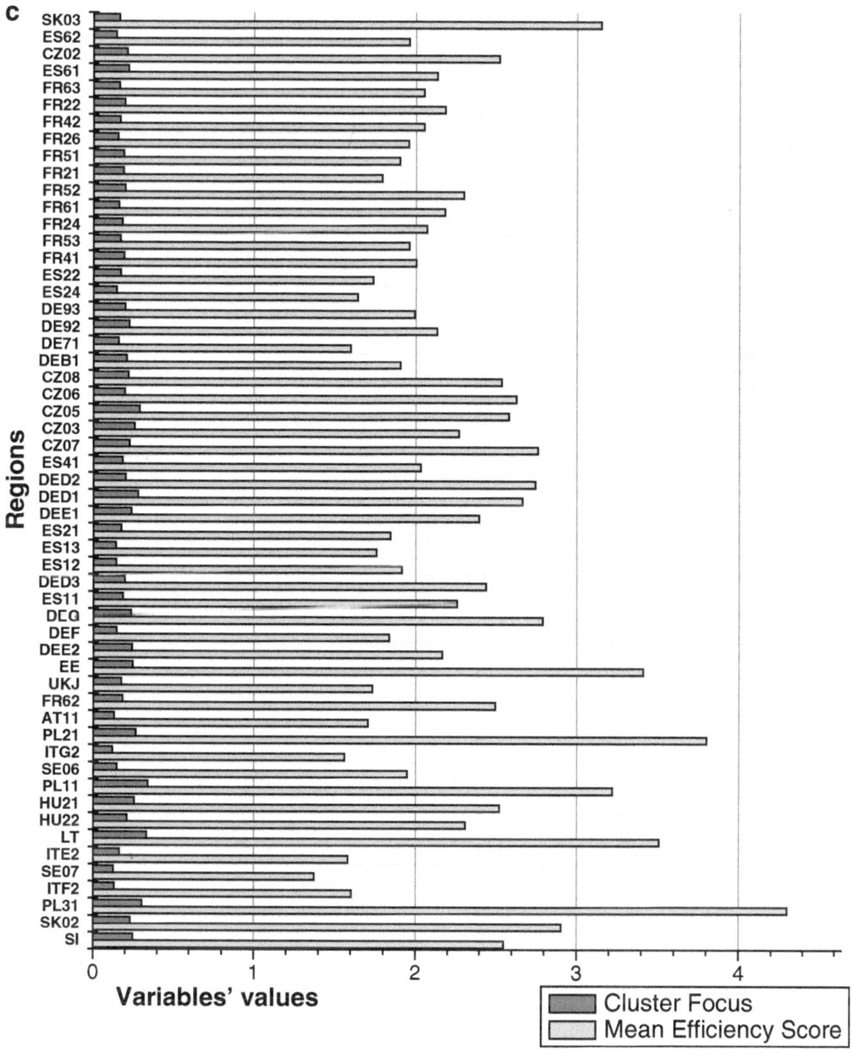

Graph 5.8 (Continued)

perhaps by increasing the intensity of involvement in the activities of the network structures.

5.3.2 *Conclusion of Findings*

With reference to the research assumptions and the realization of the aims of this dissertation – the results of the research carried out on a sample of 148 regions of the EU authorize the statement that the following hypothesis has been accepted:

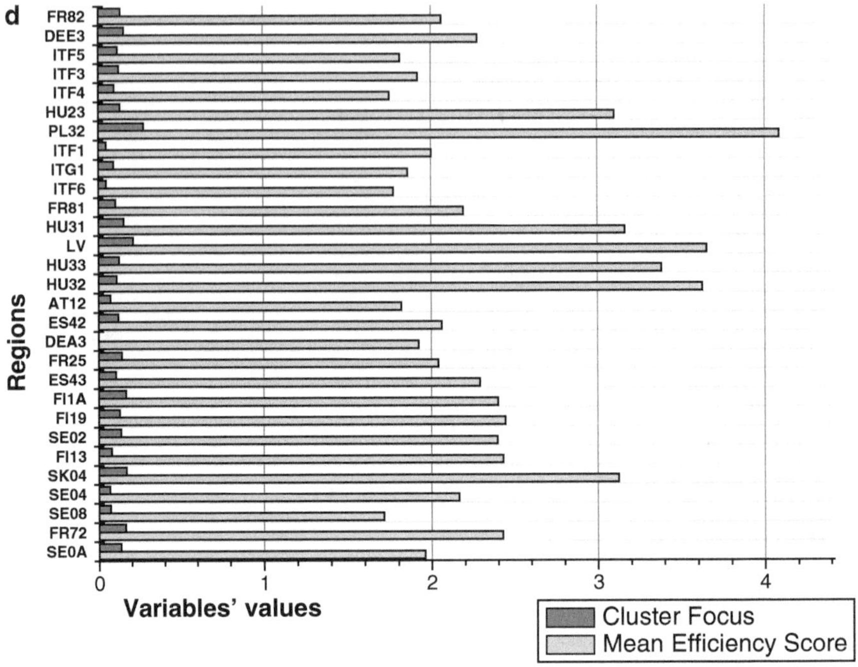

Graph 5.8 Regions clustered in groups (*k-means*). (**a**) group 1; (**b**) group 2; (**c**) group 3; (**d**) group 4

> The occurrence of the relation between the efficiency of the transformation and the degree of network interactions in EU regions that constitutes the dimension of socio-economic coherence.

In the research carried out, five DEA models were used of which each describes a chosen aspect of using resources in regions and their transformation into effects expressed in the form of the most universal indicator which is GDP per capita. As a consequence of the accepted assumptions in the construction of the analytical models on the basis of DEA methodology calculations of the indicators for particular regions of the EU were carried out. The research constituted EU regions at the level of NUTS 2 numbering 148 regions.

In the construction of the five models of efficiency groups fractional indicators were used for calculating the values of the DEA coefficients. The statistical indicators were engaged in a varying range, which means that some of them constitute variable inputs or effects in more than one model. This particularly refers to the indicator of GDP per capita which is most often availed of as a variable illustrating effects.

Table 5.6 Categorization of regions with the SOM method in four groupings

Grupa 0			Grupa 1			Grupa 2			Grupa 3		
Regions	Effectivnes indicator	Focus	Regions	Effectivnes indicator	Focus	Regions	Effectivnes indicator	Focus	Regions	Effectivnes indicator	Focus
FR62	24,954	0.1816	SI	25,479	0.2462	AT21	17,249	0.2035	SE01	12,061	0.2400
ITF5	18,151	0.1181	SE07	13,704	0.1264	PT11	24,411	0.3887	ITD5	13,432	0.3389
ITF3	19,200	0.1255	FR51	19,009	0.1885	PL22	24,400	0.2995	DE11	17,798	0.4557
ITF4	17,521	0.0963	FR42	20,522	0.1666	DE26	19,604	0.3297	ITC1	14,486	0.3316
ITC1	18,597	0.0936	FR26	19,550	0.1533	PL12	23,459	0.3062	ITD3	11,860	0.4013
ITF6	17,738	0.0465	HU22	23,082	0.2108	AT31	15,900	0.2484	ES53	11,767	0.2180
ITF1	20,023	0.0467	FR41	20,038	0.1905	AT22	17,824	0.2343	ITC2	10,004	0.1943
LV	35,530	0.2108	FR53	19,602	0.1697	AT34	13,345	0.1890	ES51	17,608	0.3989
HU23	31,020	0.1339	FR24	20,698	0.1799	PT15	16,845	0.2766	DE12	18,590	0.3349
DED2	27,443	0.2021	FR52	22,976	0.1989	AT32	11,795	0.1474	ITC4	11,744	0.4590
DEE3	22,791	0.1551	FR63	20,514	0.1630	PT18	19,280	0.2348	DE21	14,826	0.3498
HU32	36,270	0.1098	SE06	19,494	0.1470	PT16	22,952	0.3152	ITE1	14,339	0.2643
ES42	20,612	0.1202	CZ02	25,198	0.2115	DK	19,817	0.3118	DEA4	18,994	0.3508
FR25	20,406	0.1398	ITG2	15,591	0.1187	SE09	16,642	0.2021	AT33	12,609	0.2616
ES43	22,921	0.1037	ITF2	16,033	0.1315	CZ04	18,549	0.2497	DE25	17,319	0.3443
FR72	24,262	0.1622	ITE2	15,819	0.1641	ES52	19,472	0.2678	DE24	18,386	0.3445
FR61	21,813	0.1594	AT11	17,061	0.1285	DE13	20,957	0.2824	DE23	18,211	0.3878
FR82	20,640	0.1357	FR22	21,830	0.1957	FI18	18,820	0.2352	DEA5	18,274	0.3434
EE	34,096	0.2444	SK02	29,064	0.2317	PT17	17,435	0.2729	DEA1	16,551	0.3227
FR81	21,942	0.1041	PL11	32,213	0.3399	DE14	20,843	0.2767	DE27	17,944	0.3381
HU31	31,635	0.1535	LT	35,063	0.3318	SK01	14,692	0.1871	DEC	16,773	0.3768
DEA3	19,255	0.0000	HU21	25,205	0.2548	FR43	21,701	0.2858	DE22	16,144	0.2893
HU33	33,829	0.1246	ITC3	15,843	0.1498	FR83	12,859	0.1901	ITE4	13,345	0.2394
FI1A	24,002	0.1656	UKJ	17,327	0.1735	AT13	13,156	0.2169	LU	10,000	0.1873
FI13	24,295	0.0784	FR21	17,922	0.1870	MT	19,693	0.2780	**Average**	**15,128**	**0.3239**
FI19	24,437	0.1276	DE92	21,327	0.2238	DEA2	20,657	0.2829	**Regions**		**24**
SE04	21,655	0.0666	DEE1	23,961	0.2361	FR71	21,352	0.2932			
SE02	23,951	0.1354	DED3	24,392	0.1964	ITD4	13,844	0.2358			

(continued)

Table 5.6 (continued)

Grupa 0			Grupa 1			Grupa 2			Grupa 3		
Regions	Effectivnes indicator	Focus	Regions	Effectivnes indicator	Focus	Regions	Effectivnes indicator	Focus	Regions	Effectivnes indicator	Focus
SK03	31,516	0.1647	DED1	26,645	0.2782	ITE3	15,333	0.2215			
SE08	17,144	0.0701	DEB2	18,198	0.2079	ES23	15,808	0.2056			
SE0A	19,599	0.1329	DEB1	19,038	0.2093	CY	18,471	0.2497			
SK04	31,246	0.1664	DE71	15,958	0.1568	DEB3	21,914	0.2909			
ES62	19,613	0.1437	DEF	18,368	0.1454	CZ01	13,499	0.2263			
PL32	40,878	0.2759	CZ08	25,351	0.2170	DE72	21,706	0.2708			
PL31	43,006	0.3040	CZ07	27,597	0.2260	DE73	17,050	0.2533			
PL21	38,024	0.2645	CZ06	26,257	0.1968	FR23	20,503	0.2510			
AT12	18,208	0.0724	CZ05	25,800	0.2876	DE91	20,714	0.3431			
Average	**25,384**	**0.1388**	CZ03	22,703	0.2563	DE94	17,198	0.2922			
Regions		**37**	DEE2	21,662	0.2412	**Average**	**18,414**	**0.2591**			
			DE93	19,931	0.1979	**Regions**		**38**			
			DEG	27,900	0.2350						
			ES11	22,589	0.1834						
			ES41	20,309	0.1827						
			ES21	18,446	0.1759						
			ES13	17,587	0.1404						
			ES12	19,140	0.1432						
			ES22	17,349	0.1701						
			ES24	16,391	0.1455						
			ES61	21,351	0.2210						
			Average	**21,369**	**0.1966**						
			Regions:		**49**						

As a result of the DEA methodology used a significant correlation was noticed between the particular models of the following: M1, M3, M4 (and the comparative model) the synthetic M5, while in the case of the M2 model no significant correlation was observed.

In the subsequent parts of the research procedure aimed at verifying the main hypothesis of this dissertation, new characteristics were introduced to the set of variables serving the marking out of the efficiency of regions and their recategorization was carried out. The implementation of new variables was aimed at identifying the network phenomena occurring in regions and the definition of their approximate impact or relation on efficiency.

For the purpose of realizing aims of the second stage the k-means method was used. The categorization with the aid of these methods was carried out by the acceptance of the assumptions regarding the number of groups and subsequently through the implementation of the optimising algorithm which leads to the standardization of the composition of particular groups. At the end of the procedures carried out standardized groups were formed with regard to the variables used. The innovativeness of availing of this methodology in the case of the research carried out in this dissertation involves the fact that the variable "network" is used for the categorization of the variation between regions in the EU.

In this dissertation it was assumed that for the purpose of regional clustering, two variables were used as follows: the parameter of efficiency and the parameter of networking.

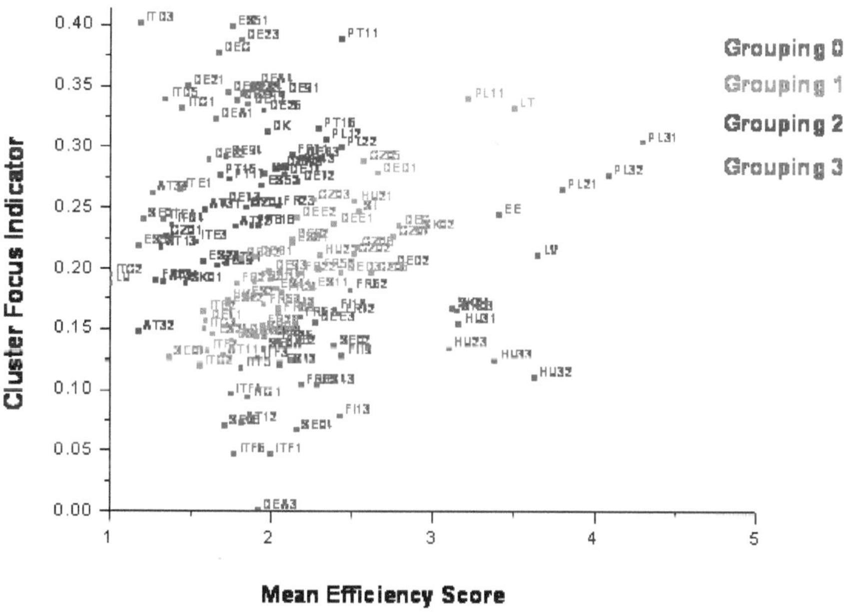

Graph 5.9 (Continued)

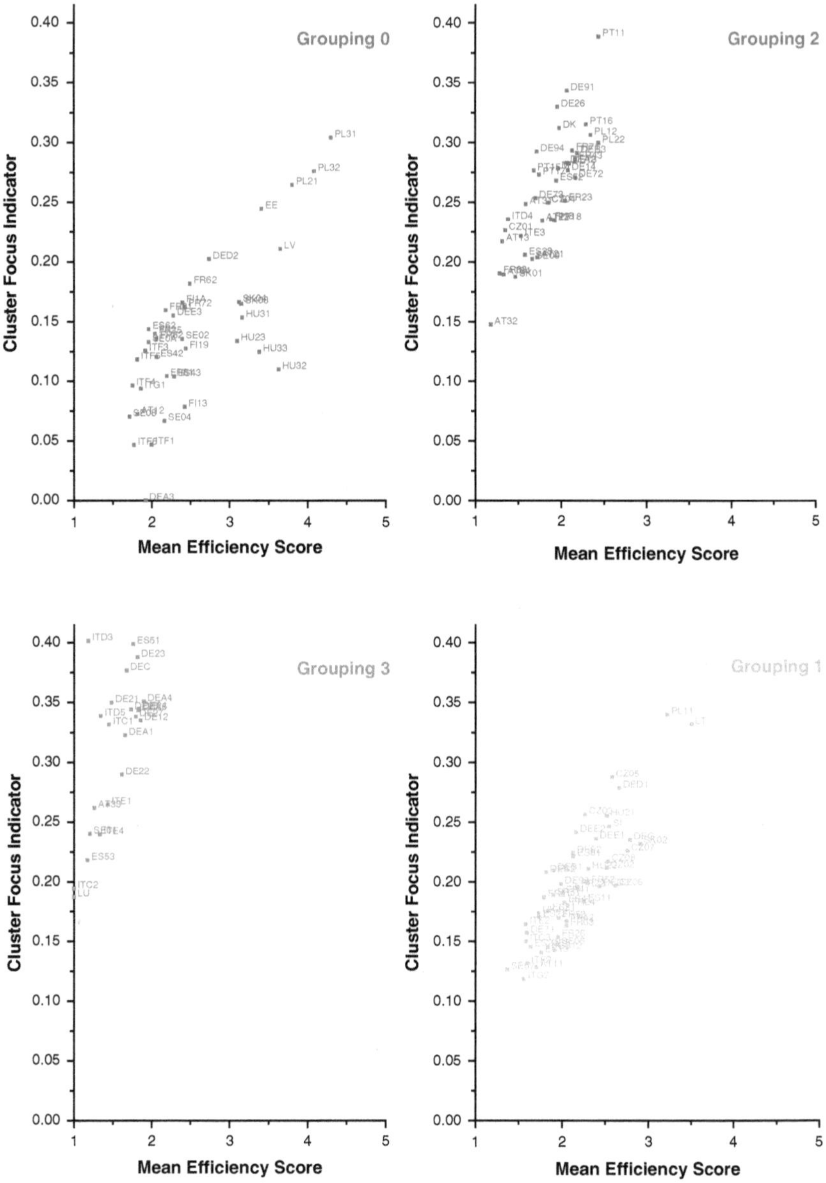

Graph 5.9 Clustering of EU regions by *Self Organizing Map* method. (**a**) position of four groups

Table 5.7 Set of fundamental statistics of the results of categorization with the SOM method and the "k-means" method

		SOM clustering statistics								K-means clustering statistics					
		Mean	Standard deviation	Standard elrror	Min	Max	Range			Mean	Standard deviation	Standard error	Min	Max	Range
Gr0	Mean Efficiency Score	25,384	0.7237	0.1190	17,144	43,006	25,862	**Gr4**	Mean Efficiency Score	24,095	0.6555	0.1217	17,144	40,878	23,734
	Cluster Focus	0.1388	0.0646	0.0106	0.0000	0.3040	0.3040		Cluster Focus	0.1197	0.0530	0.0098	0.0000	0.2759	0.2759
Gr1	Mean Efficiency Score	21,369	0.4514	0.0645	13,704	35,063	21,359	**Gr3**	Mean Efficiency Score	22,791	0.5915	0.0798	13,704	43,006	29,302
	Cluster Focus	0.1966	0.0496	0.0071	0.1187	0.3399	0.2212		Cluster Focus	0.1989	0.0508	0.0069	0.1187	0.3399	0.2212
Gr2	Mean Efficiency Score	18,414	0.3352	0.0544	11,795	24,411	12,616	**Gr1**	Mean Efficiency Score	18,389	0.3267	0.0517	11,795	24,411	12,616
	Cluster Focus	0.2591	0.0489	0.0079	0.1474	0.3887	0.2413		Cluster Focus	0.2613	0.0533	0.0084	0.1474	0.3989	0.2515
Gr3	Mean Efficiency Score	15,128	0.2931	0.0598	10,000	18,994	0.8994	**Gr2**	Mean Efficiency Score	15,054	0.2888	0.0590	10,000	18,994	0.8994
	Cluster Focus	0.3239	0.0743	0.0152	0.1873	0.4590	0.2717		Cluster Focus	0.3135	0.0805	0.0164	0.1498	0.4590	0.3092

The average indicator of the efficiency of a region was calculated at the outset with the "DEA index." The average indicator of efficiency indicated the general range of efficiency of the region thus constituting a specific "ranking" of regions analysed with regard to various aspects of efficiency.

A considerable problem proved to be the assignment of a significant indicator of networking and following literary study and analysis of the accessibility of statistical data at the level of regions in NUTS 2, a choice was made with regard to the indicator referring to employment in sectoral clusters occurring in particular regions (Focus). It was acknowledged that this indicator best reflects the occurrence of network structures in the economy of regions.

On the basis of the research carried out it was stated that correlation exists between the two variables (the DEA index and the indicator of networking – Focus). A higher efficiency of a region is associated with a higher indicator of networking in a region. It is therefore possible to refer to the hypothesis provided and state that a high level of network structures in a region is connected with a high efficiency of the given region as shown in Table 5.8. This was the question asked in the research and in the hypothesis provided in this dissertation.

For the purpose of verifying the results acquired a regrouping of the regions was carried out with the aid of the same criteria but with the implementation of modifications to the methodology applied. The method of *Self Organizing Maps (SOM)* was applied for this purpose.

The verification of the research results with the SOM method confirmed the significance of the research results acquired.

An illustration of the geographical arrangement of the particular regions has been presented below (Map 5.1) with regard to their efficiency in the transformation and the indicator of network interaction. The regions of group 2, or in other words, the most efficient regions and with simultaneously the highest indicator of networking include the main regions of the northern parts of Italy and the central parts of Germany.

On the basis of the aforementioned maps it is possible to observe that the regions with the highest indicators (group 2) are located within geographical proximity of each other. The trend of geographical proximity of the regions observed constitutes an additional result of the research carried out and may constitute a signal for further analysis with the aim of identifying the network interactions between regions of this part of the EU. Simultaneously, due to the lack of some statistical data at the level of NUTS 2 it was not possible to prepare maps that included all the regions.

Table 5.8 Illustration of regional efficiency and networking relations (k-means)

Factor/group	Group 1	Group 2	Group 3	Group 4
Index DEA	18,389	15,054	22,791	24,095
Focus	0.2613	0.3135	0.1989	0.1197

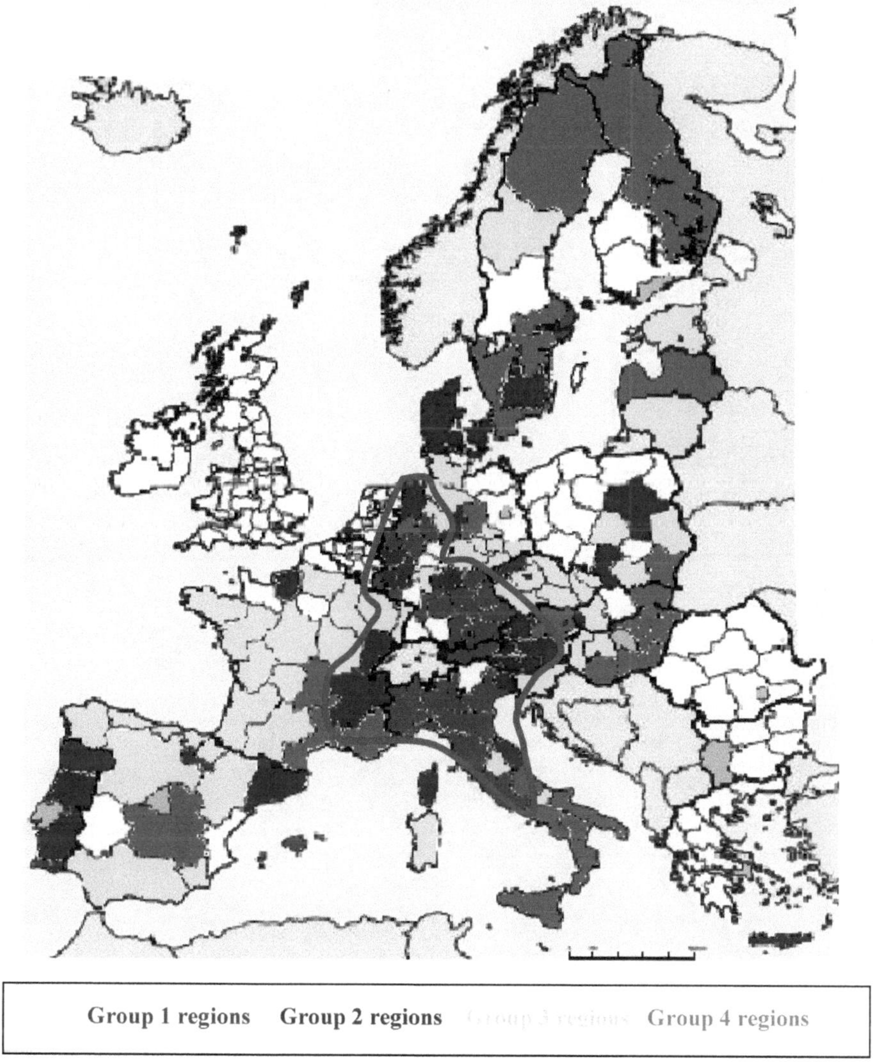

Map 5.1 Presentation of the geographical arrangement of particular groups of regions with regard to the *Index DEA* and *Focus* indicators with the aid of the *k-means* method

The continuation of research in the socio-economic coherence of regions in the EU is important from the point of view of the strategy of the EU and the policy of allocating funds. Analysis in the area of the development of network interaction in particular regions of the EU is of significance for policies in the case of the growth of competitiveness and innovativeness of the EU in the area of endogenic sustainable growth, as well as in the area of global competition.

Bibliography

4th Report on economic and social cohesion, The European Commission, 2007

A Practical Guide to Cluster Development. Department of Trade and Industry, London

Abramowitz M (1989) *Thinking about Growth*. Cambridge University Press, Cambridge

Aghion P, Howitt P, Brant-Collett M, García-Peñalosa C (eds) (1998) Endogenous growth theory. MIT, Cambridge, MA

Andersson T (2004) *The Cluster Policies Whitebook*. IKED, Malmo

Arrow K (1962) *The Economic Implications of Learning by Doing*. Rev Econ Stud 29:155–173

Article 10 ERDF innovative actions. EC, Brussels, 2000

Asheim BT, Isaksen A (2000) *Localised Knowledge, Interactive Learning and Innovation: Between Regional Networks and Global Corporations*. In: Vante E, Taylor M (eds) *The Networked Firm in a Global World*: Small Firms in New Environment. Aldershot, Ashgate

Aumayr Ch (2007) *European Region Types in EU-25*. Eur J Comp Econ 4(2):109–147

Banker RD, Charnes A, Cooper WW (1984) *Some Models for Estimating Technical and Scale Inefficiencies in Data Envelopment Analysis*. Manag Sci 30(9):1078–1092

Becattini G (1990) The Marshallian Industrial Districts as Socio-Economic Notion. In: Pyke F, Becattini G, Sengerberger W (eds) *Industrial Districts and Inter-firm Cooperation in Italy*. International Institute for Labour Studies, Geneva

Blien U, Rueb F, Werner D, Wolf K (2006) Classification of Regional Labour Markets at the Nuts 3 Level in Germany. Paper presented at the 46th congress of the European Regional Science Association, Greece, http://www.prd.uth.gr/ersa2006

Boosting Innovation. The Cluster Approach. OECD, 1999

Breschi S, Malerba F (2007) *Clusters, Networks, and Innovation: Research Results and New Directions*. Oxford University Press, Oxford

Brodnicki T, Szultka S, Tamowicz P (2004) *Polityka wspierania klastrów. Najlepsze praktyki. Rekomendacje dla Polski*, Niebieskie Księgi, Rekomendacje, 11, IBNGR, Gdańsk

Business Clusters in the UK. Department of Trade and Industry, London, 2001

Cainelli G, Zoboli R (eds) (2004) *Marshallian Industrial Districts. The Evolution of Industrial Districts: Changing Governance, Innovation and Internationalisation of Local Capitalism in Italy*. Physica Verlag, Heidelberg

Castells M (2001) *La ciudad de la Nueva Economia*. Papeles de Poblacio´n, enero-marzo, 27/2001, Toluca

Charnes A, Cooper WW, Rhodes E (1978) *Measuring the Efficiency of Decision Making Units*. Eur J Oper Res 2:429–444

Charnes A, Cooper WW, Lewin AY, Seiford LM (1994) *Data Envelopment Analysis: Theory, Methodology and Application*. Kluwer, Boston, MA

Cities and Regions in the New Learning Economy. OECD, Paris, 2001

Cluster Based Economic Development: A Key to Regional Competitiveness. EDA, 1997

Coelli T, Prasada Rao DS, Battese GE (2001) *An introduction to efficiency and productivity analysis*. Kluwer Academic Publisher, London

Cooke P (2006) *Bliskość, wiedza i powstawanie innowacji*. Studia Regionalne i Lokalne 2(24)

Cooke P (2001) *Clusters as Key Determinants of Economic Growth: The Example of Biotechnology*. In: Mariussen (ed) *Cluster Policies – Cluster Development*? Nordregio Report 2001:2, Stockholm

Cooke P (1996) *The New Wave of Regional Innovation Networks: Analysis, Characteristics and Strategy*. Small Bus Econ 8:159–171

Cooper WW, Seiford LM, Tone K. *Data envelopment analysis: a comprehensive text with models, applications, references and DEA-solver software*. Kluwer, Dordrecht

Cross RL, Israelit SB (2000) *Strategic learning in a knowledge economy: individual, collective and organizational learning process*. Butterworth-Heinemann, Boston, MA

Davenport T, Leibold M, Voelpl S (2006) *Strategic Management in the Innovation Economy*. Publicis, Erlangen

Debreu G (1951) *The Coefficient of Recourse Utilization*. Econometrica 19:273–292

Derek HC Chen, Dahlman CJ (2006) *The Knowledge Economy, The KAM Methodology and World Bank Operations*. The World Bank, Washington, DC

Enlargement, two years after: an economic evaluation. European Economy, *European Economy* Nr 24/2006

European Innovation Scoreboard 2005

Fare R, Grosskopf S, Lovell CAK (1985) *The Measurement of Efficiency of Production*. Kluwer-Nijhoff, Boston, MA

Farell MJ (1956) *The Measurement of Productive Efficiency*. J R Stat Soc Ser A 120:253–281

First progress report on cohesion. EC, Luxemburg, 2002

Florida R (2000) *The Learning Region*. In: Acs ZJ (ed) *Regional Innovation, Knowledge and Global Change*. Pinter, New York, NY

Francik A (2003) *Sterowanie procesami innowacyjnymi w organizacji*. Wydawnictwo AE, Kraków

Fried HO, Knox Lovell CA, Schmidt SS (1993) *The Measurement of Productive Efficiency Techniques and Applications*. Oxford University Press, New York, Oxford

Gancarczyk J, Gancarczyk M (2002) *Konkurencyjność skupisk przemysłu (clusters) – od korzyści zewnętrznych do korzyści sieci*. Studia Regionalne i Lokalne 2–3

Goldberg I (2004) *Polska a gospodarka oparta na wiedzy. W kierunku zwiększania konkurencyjności Polski w Unii Europejskiej*. Bank Światowy, Waszyngton

Green Paper on Innovation, Supplement, 1995 Brussels, 1996

Greunz L (2005) *Intra- and Inter-Regional Knowledge Spillovers: Evidence from European Regions*. Eur Plann Stud 13(3):449–473

Grosse TG (2002) *Przegląd koncepcji teoretycznych rozwoju regionalnego*. Studia Regionalne i Lokalne 1(8)

Hoen A (2001) Clusters: determinants and effects. CPB Netherlands Bureau for Economic Policy Analysis, Netherlands

http://www.cis.hut.fi/~sami/thesis/

http://www.cis.hut.fi/~sami/thesis/node25.html

http://www.cis.hut.fi/~sami/thesis/node26.html

Innovative Clusters. Drivers of National Innovation Systems. OECD, 2001

Innowacje i transfer technologii. Słownik pojęć, PARP, Warszawa, 2005

Innovative Networks. Co-operation in National Innovation Systems. OECD, 2001

Jelonek D (2004) *Zarządzanie wiedzą jako czynnik wspomagający wdrożenie zmian organizacyjnych*. (Knowledge management as an organizational change factor) Scientific Works of Wrocław Academy of Economics 1011. Wrocław

Karlsson Ch (eds) (2008) *Handbook of research on cluster theory*. Edward Elgar, Cheltenham

Keeble D (1976) Industrial location and Planning in the UK. Taylor & Francis, London

Keeble D, Wilkinson F (1999) *Collective Learning and Knowledge Development in the Evolution of Regional Clusters of High Technology SMSEs in Europe*. Reg Stud 33(4):295–303

Ketels Ch, Sölvell Ö (2006) *Clusters in the EU-10 new member countries*, EUROPE INNOVA Cluster Mapping

Les action structureles 2000–2006, Commentaires et Reglement, Commission europeenne, Luxemburg, 1999

Lundvall BA, Borrás S (1997) *The globalising learning economy: implications for innovation policy*. Report based on contributions from seven projects under the TSER programme, Commission of the European Union

Lundvall BA (1992) *National Systems of Innovation: Towards a Theory of Innovation and Interactive learning*. Printer, London

Lundvall BA (1998) *Why Study National Systems and National Styles of Innovation*? Tech Anal Strat Manag 10(4):407–421

de Ard-Pieter M (2004) *The Network Economy*. Edward Elgar, Cheltenham

Marelli E (2007) *Regional Employment Dynamics in the EU: Structural Outlook, Co- Movements, Clusters and Common Shocks*. In: Caroleo F, Destefanis S (eds) The European labour market. Physica Verlag, Heidelberg

Morgan K (1997) *The Learning Region: Institutions, Innovation and Regional Renewal*. Reg Stud 31(5):491–503

Nelson R, Winter S (1982) *An evolutionary theory of economic exchange*. Harvard University Press, Cambridge

Nowicka Skowron M, Pachura P, Nitkiewicz T, Kozak M (2006) *Regional Intellectual Capital: Disentangling a New Concept*. In: Stachowicz J (ed) Intelectual capital management in regional pro-innovative networks. Exit, Warszawa

Okoń-Horodyńska E (2000) *Jak budować regionalne systemy innowacji*. Instytut Badań nad Gospodarką Rynkową, Warszawa

Olejniczak K (2003) Apetyt na grona? *Koncepcja gron oraz koncepcje bliskoznaczne w teorii i praktyce rozwoju regionalnego*. Studia Regionalne i Lokalne 2(12)

OECD and Eurostat (2005) *Oslo Manual. Guidelines for Collecting and Interpreting Innovation Data*, 3rd edn. OECD and Eurostat, Paris

Pachura P (2006) *System Thinking and Global Challenges*. ISI Pierrard, HEC du Luxemburg, Virton

Pachura P, Kozak M (2006) *Kapitał społeczny w regionalnych sieciach innowacyjnych*. In: Stachowicz J, Straszak A, Walukiewicz S (eds) Badania operacyjne i systemowe. Exit, Warszawa

Pachura P, Nowicka-Skowron M (2007) *Cohesion in the EU – the Comparative Analysis*. In: Lescroart R, Pachura P, Nitkiewicz T (eds) *Interdisciplinary Approach to Sustainable Development*. Haute Ecole Catholique du Luxemburg, Virton

Perugini C, Signorelli M (2004) *Employment Performance and Convergence in the European Countries and Regions*. Eur J Comp Econ 1(2):243–278

Pollock R (2003) *The regional dimension*. ECORYS-NEI Strategy and Entrepreneurship, Rotterdam

Porter ME (1998) *Clusters and the new economics of competition*. Harv Bus Rev 76(6):77–90

Porter ME (2001) *Porter o konkurencji*. PWE, Warszawa

Prigogine I, Stengers I (1984) *Order out of chaos: a mans dialogue with nature*. Bantam, New York, Bantam

Principeaux resultats du tableau de bord europeen de l'innovation 2001. In: Innovation & Transfer Technplogique, CE, DG Entreprises, Luxemburg, 2001

Pyka A (2002) *Innovation networks in economics*. Eur J Innovat Manag 5(3):152–163

Ricardo D (1957) *The principles of political economy and taxation*. Warsaw, polish edition

Rola kapitału społecznego w tworzeniu wartości przedsiębiorstwa. Humanizacja Pracy 2–3/1999

Romer P (1990) *Endogenous Technological Change*. J Polit Econ 98(5):S71–S102

Rózga Luter R (2004) *Gospodarka oparta na wiedzy a rozwój regionalny na przykładzie Regionu Środkowego Meksyku*. Studia Regionalne i Lokalne 1(15)

Salmi P, Blomqvist K, Ahola J, Kyläheiko K (2001) *Industrial districts and regional development: Towards a knowledge-based view*. Working Papers 7, Lappeenranta University of Technology, Lappeenranta

Scott AJ (1993) *Technopolis. High-technology Industry and Regional Development in Southern California*. University of California Press, Berkeley, CA

Sixieme rapport periodique sur la situation et l'evolution socio-economique des regions, Troisieme partie: situation et tendances dans les region aidees, DG XVI, Luksemburg, 1998

Skowron-Grabowska B, Otola I (2006) *Centra logistyczne a działalność jednostek samorządu terytorialnego* (Logistics center and local authorities). In: Markowski T (ed) *Rola centrów logistycznych w rozwoju gospodarczym i przestrzennym kraju* (The role of logistics center in spatial management), vol 225. Polish Academy of Science, Warsaw

Sławecki B (2005) *Kapitał społeczny organizacji a koszty transakcyjne*. In: Januszek H (ed) *Kapitał społeczny we wspólnotach*, zeszyty naukowe, vol 58. Wydawnictwo Akademii Ekonomicznej w Poznaniu, Poznań

Smith A (2008) *Inquiry into the Nature and Causes of the Wealth of Nationes*. Wydawnictwo Naukowe PWN, Warsaw

Stachowicz J (2006) *Modele procesów rozwoju współczesnego przedsiębiorstwa: geneza, praktyczna użyteczność*, Zeszyty Naukowe PŚ Organizacja i Zarządzanie, z. 37 Gliwice

Ståhle P, Grönroos M (2000) *Dynamic Intellectual Capital. Knowledge Management in Theory and Practice*. WSOY, Vantaa

Ståhle P (1998) *Supporting a system's capacity for self-renewal*. Yliopistopaino, Helsinki

Stawasz E (2005) *Determinanty działalności innowacyjnej*. In: *Innowacje i transfer technologii. Słownik pojęć*. PARP, Warszawa

Stawasz E, Głodek P, Matusiak KB (2006) *Identyfikacja zmian zachodzących pomiędzy podmiotami w regionalnym systemie innowacji w województwie śląskim w latach 2002–2006*, dokument opracowany w ramach projektu "Jednostka Zarządzająca Regionalnym Systemem Innowacji w województwie śląskim", Katowice

Szultka S, Tamowicz P, Mackiewicz M (2004) *Regionalne Strategie i Systemy Innowacji. Najlepsze Praktyki. Rekomendacje dla Polski*, Niebieskie Księgi, Nr 12. IBNGR, Gdańsk 2004

The Future of the Global Economy. Towards a Long Boom? OECD, Paris, 1999

OECD (1996) *The Knowledge-based Economy*. OECD, Paris

The Learning Region: Institutions, Innovation and Regional Renewal. Reg Stud 31(5) 1997

Unity, solidarity, diversity for Europe, its people and its territory, second report on economic and social cohesion, EC, Luxemburg, 2001

Weyman-Jones T (2003) *Yardstick competition and efficiency benchmarking in electricity distribution*. In: Hunt LC (ed) *Energy in a Competitive Market*. Edward Elgar, Cheltenham

FSC
www.fsc.org
MIX
Papier | Fördert gute Waldnutzung
FSC® C083411

Kolibri 360 GmbH
Ferdinand-Jühlke-Straße 7
99095 Erfurt, Deutschland
produktsicherheit@kolibri360.de